PILGRIM'S
PRAYER BOOK

LIVING CLASSICS
JOHN BUNYAN

PILGRIM'S PRAYER BOOK

A Month of Meditations on Prayer
by the Author of PILGRIM'S PROGRESS

Edited by
Louis Gifford Parkhurst, Jr.

Tyndale House Publishers, Inc.
Wheaton, Illinois

The text of Bunyan's work has been completely
revised and updated for the modern reader.

Scripture quotations are from *The Holy Bible, New
International Version*. Copyright © 1978 by New
York International Bible Society. Used by permission
of Zondervan Bible Publishers.

First printing, January 1986
Library of Congress Catalog Card Number 85-51596
ISBN 0-8423-4933-2

Prayer is a sincere, sensible, affectionate pouring out of the heart or soul to God, through Christ, in the strength and assistance of the Holy Spirit, for such things as God has promised, or according to the Word of God, for the good of the church, with submission in faith to the will of God.

John Bunyan
Bedford Prison
1662

CONTENTS

THE LIFE OF JOHN BUNYAN

John Bunyan was born in 1628 at Elstow, near Bedford, in England. The son of poor parents, he had no formal education and probably acquired his grasp of the English language from reading the Bible. He fought on the side of Cromwell's Roundheads (Puritans) in the English Civil War. In 1649 he married, and for her dowry his wife gave him two devotional books. His interest in the spiritual life increased, and in 1653 he joined an Independent church at Bedford.

Not long after this he began to preach, but in 1660 he was called before the local magistrate for preaching without a license. The magistrate insisted that Bunyan cease preaching. Bunyan refused, and as a result he spent most of the next twelve years in prison. He was, like many other faithful believers of his age, a victim of the change that occurred when Cromwell's Puritan government was replaced by the restored Stuart dynasty. The Stuart King Charles II wanted conformity in the churches in England, and Bunyan and others refused to conform to a form of worship that could only follow the *Book of Common Prayer*.

During his imprisonment, Bunyan wrote his most famous works: the classic allegory *The Pilgrim's Progress* (1678, 1684); his spiritual autobiography *Grace Abounding to the Chief of Sinners* (1666); and the allegory *The Holy War* (1682). *Pilgrim's Progress* was widely read in Britain and colonial America, and it continues to be popular. Bunyan wrote several other books and tracts while in prison, including the discourse on prayer adapted in the present volume.

After his release from prison in 1672, Bunyan spent most of his time preaching and evangelizing in the Bedford area. He died in 1688. His life and writings have established his reputation as a master of clear, simple English prose that has impressed generations of Christians and literary critics.

INTRODUCTION

A poor uneducated tinker, John Bunyan was imprisoned for preaching in public and working for religious freedom in England. From his lonely prison cell, Bunyan learned how to pray, and it was from that same cell that he was inspired to write his devotional classics.

In 1662, he wrote his thoughts on prayer, thoughts forged on the anvil of religious persecution. His wife had struggled in vain to win his release from Bedford Prison in 1661, and he faced an uncertain future—execution or more years in prison. He took comfort from two books in his possession during the writing of these meditations on prayer: the *Bible* and *Foxe's Book of Martyrs*. (Foxe's book, popular for centuries, told of the faithful Protestants martyred during the reign of the Catholic queen Mary Tudor—"Bloody Mary.") Bunyan learned from these writings that the only way to glorify God in his sufferings, even if he were destined for the scaffold, was to pray often and pray deeply. What he learned from his prayers he carefully wrote down, and then he passed his sheets of manuscript through the prison bars to encourage his wife and those facing persecution, prison, and death.

Bunyan, like other Christians who had separated themselves from the Church of England, wanted Christians to be able to preach and pray freely. The authorities in the Church of England wanted people's religious life to center around the *Book of Common Prayer,* which contained prayers for every day of the year and for special occasions. Bunyan and other independents felt that each individual Christian should be guided in his prayers by the Holy Spirit, not by the prayers and rituals in the *Book of Common Prayer.* Bunyan never said the *Book of Common Prayer* was bad in itself—he said (as the following pages will show) that any Christian should be allowed to pray whenever and however the Spirit leads. To pray, for Bunyan, meant more than repeating words out of a book. The Church of England disagreed, which is why Bunyan wrote his books inside a prison cell.

I have edited his writings on prayer into these thirty-one daily meditations, and I have updated the language for the modern reader. Following each meditation, I have written my own prayer. I hope my prayers will encourage you to pray your own prayers, applying Bunyan's principles to your situation. You will find Bunyan's meditations to be simple, direct, and rich in Scripture and its application.

I have adopted Bunyan's purpose in editing these meditations. We want you to pray in both spirit and mind. We want to encourage you to pray according to the Scriptures and under the Holy Spirit's leading. As Bunyan condemned the mechanicalness and heartlessness that can attend the use of many prayer books or prayer techniques, so we hope that the *Pilgrim's Prayer Book* will grant you greater insight and freedom of expression in your personal relationship with God through Jesus Christ.

For the sake of His Kingdom,
L. G. Parkhurst, Jr.
Christian Life Study Center
1985

MEDITATION ONE
TRUE PRAYER

PRAYER is an ordinance of God. Prayer is commanded by him to be used in public and in private. Prayer brings those who have the spirit of supplication into a great familiarity with God. Therefore, prayer has been ordained by God as a means of our growing in a personal relationship with him.

When prayer is prevalent in action, it acquires great things from God, both for the person who prays and for those who are prayed for. Prayer opens the heart of God, and it is the means by which the soul, though empty, is filled by God. By prayer the Christian can open his heart to God, as to a friend, and obtain fresh evidence of God's friendship with him.

I might spend many words in distinguishing between public and private prayer. I might also distinguish between silent prayer and prayer that is spoken aloud. Something also might be said regarding the differences between the gifts and the graces of prayer. But I have chosen instead to make it my business to show you only the very *heart* of prayer, without which all your lifting up of hands and eyes and voices will be to no purpose at all. We must know what the Scripture teaches, for Paul wrote giving us an example, "I will pray with my spirit" (1 Cor. 14:15).

The method that I shall use in this book will tell you: *first,* what true prayer is; *second;* what it is to pray with the Spirit; *third,* what it is to pray with the Spirit and with the mind; and *fourth,* what are some uses and applications of what I have explained about prayer.

True prayer is a sincere, sensible, affectionate pouring out of the heart or soul to God, through Christ, in the strength and assistance of the Holy Spirit, for such things as God has promised, or according to the Word of God, for the good of the church, with submission in faith to the will of God.

In this definition are seven things which I must discuss in detail in the following pages. First, I will show that prayer must be sincere. Second, prayer must be sensible— that is, *aware*—of God's majesty and our sin. Third, prayer must be an affectionate—deeply felt—pouring out of the soul to God, through Christ.* Fourth, effective prayer must be by the strength and assistance of the Spirit. Fifth, for your prayers to be answered according to the will of God, you must pray for such things as God has promised, or according to his Word, the Bible. Sixth, your prayers should not be selfish, but should keep in view the good of other Christians—the church. Seventh, you should always pray in faith, with submission to the will of God.

---

*Bunyan frequently uses the words *sensible* and *affectionate* in his writings. Generally, when he speaks of *sensible* prayer, he refers to prayer involving our *sense* of God's majesty and our own unworthiness. The person praying must not merely repeat words, but must deeply feel—*sense*—God's majesty and mercy and man's sinfulness. *Affectionate* means "having to do with the affections"—*affections* being the seventeenth-century term for what we today call *feelings* or *the heart* or *emotions.* For Bunyan, prayer must be *affectionate*—that is, it must involve a person's deep feelings, his emotions.

PRAYER

O God, the pressures of my busy life weigh upon me, and I confess that I have not taken the time to develop a deep familiarity with you. I have not really opened my heart to you, nor have I taken the time to know by experience the openness of your heart to me. Help me over these next several days to take the time to learn about true prayer from John Bunyan, a master of prayer, who knew what it was to learn of you behind prison walls, and help me also pray. Help me to pray in order to know you better. Help me to pray so I might be empowered to witness before those who need to accept the truth of the gospel of your precious Son. For his sake I pray. Amen.

MEDITATION TWO
SINCERE PRAYER

MEDITATION TWO

SINCERE PRAYER

PRAYER is a SINCERE, sensible, affectionate pouring out of the heart or soul to God, through Christ, in the strength and assistance of the Holy Spirit, for such things as God has promised, or according to the Word of God, for the good of the church, with submission in faith to the will of God.

For the first part of this explanation, prayer is a *sincere* pouring out of the heart or soul to God. Sincerity is such a grace that it runs through all the graces of God in us. Sincerity should run through all the actions of a Christian and have the sway in them. If sincerity is not in the Christian's actions, then his actions are not approved by God.

This is true of prayer, of which particularly David speaks when he mentions his own prayers: "I cried out to him [the Lord] with my mouth; his praise was on my tongue. If I had cherished sin in my heart, the Lord would not have listened; but God has surely listened and heard my voice in prayer" (Ps. 66:17-19).

Part of the exercise of prayer is sincerity, for without sincerity God does not look upon it as a prayer in the good sense: "I said to the LORD, 'You are my Lord; apart from you I have no good thing.' As for the saints who are in

6

the land, they are the glorious ones in whom is all my delight. The sorrows of those will increase who run after other gods. I will not pour out their libations of blood or take up their names on my lips" (Ps. 16:2-4). "Then you will call upon me and come and pray to me, and I will listen to you. You will seek me and find me when you seek me with all your heart" (Jer. 29:12, 13).

The lack of sincerity makes the Lord reject our prayers. In the prophets, God said, "They do not cry out to me from their hearts," that is, in sincerity, "but wail upon their beds" (Hos. 7:14). They prayed for a show of hypocrisy, to be seen by men and applauded for their loud prayers.

Christ commended Nathanael for his sincerity: "When Jesus saw Nathanael approaching, he said of him, 'Here is a true Israelite, in whom there is nothing false' " (John 1:47). Probably this good man was pouring out his soul to God in prayer in a sincere and unfeigned spirit. The prayer that has sincerity in it as one of the principal ingredients is the prayer that God hears. Thus, "The LORD detests the sacrifice of the wicked, but the prayer of the upright pleases him" (Prov. 15:8).

Why must sincerity be one of the essentials of prayer which is accepted by God? Because sincerity carries your soul in all simplicity to open your heart to God and to tell him the case plainly and without equivocation. Sincerity in prayer motivates the heart to condemn its sin plainly, without concealing the facts, intentions, or feelings under false excuses and pretenses.

When we pray from the heart, we cry to God heartily without complimenting ourselves or praising our righteousness. The Lord declared to Jeremiah the prophet: " 'I have surely heard Ephraim's moaning: "You disciplined me like an unruly calf, and I have been disciplined. Restore

7

me, and I will return, because you are the LORD my God. After I strayed, I repented; after I came to understand, I beat my breast. I was ashamed and humiliated because I bore the disgrace of my youth" ' " (Jer. 31:18, 19).

Sincerity is the same in a person whether he is in a corner all alone or before the face of the whole world. Sincerity does not know how to wear two different masks, one for an appearance before men and another for a short span in a corner. It is not lip-labor that God regards. It is the heart that God looks at, and it is the sincere heart from which prayer comes. God regards prayer from his children when it is accompanied by sincerity.

PRAYER

O Lord, my God, may I be found of you as Jesus found Nathanael along the way, in sincere and in utterly devoted prayer to you. I confess that some of my motives for prayer have been selfish and self-seeking. I confess that I have often not taken the time to examine my heart and open it completely before you in prayer. Instead, I have come making known only the things I want you to do for me. I bow before you now, O Lord, in humble submission, and I ask you to make in me a clean heart and put a right spirit within me. I come to you in complete sincerity that I would be known of you and you would be known of me, that your Son might commend me when we meet, that there would be nothing false in me, that I might also feel free to pray in the Savior's name knowing that I am cleansed by his blood. Amen.

MEDITATION THREE
HOW TO PRAY FOR MERCY

PRAYER is a sincere, SENSIBLE, affectionate pouring out of the heart or soul to God, through Christ, in the strength and assistance of the Holy Spirit, for such things as God has promised, or according to the Word of God, for the good of the church, with submission in faith to the will of God.

Prayer is not, as many take it to be, just a few babbling, prating, complimentary expressions, but a *sensible feeling* in the heart, an awareness of what God is and what we are. Prayer is sensible of many diverse things. Sometimes we pray with a sense—awareness—of sin, sometimes with a sense of mercy needed or received, and sometimes with a sense that God is ready to give us mercy.

Often in prayer there is a sense of the need of mercy, by reason of our understanding the danger of sin. The soul feels, and from feeling it sighs, groans, and breaks in the heart. Right prayer can bubble up out of the heart pressed with grief and bitterness. When Hannah prayed for a child, the Scripture says, "In bitterness of soul Hannah wept much and prayed to the Lord" (1 Sam. 1:10). And the Lord heard her prayer and she conceived and gave birth to the great prophet Samuel.

10

"I am worn out calling for help; my throat is parched. My eyes fail, looking for my God," cried David (Ps. 69:3). David roars, weeps, faints at heart, and fails at the eyes: "I am feeble and utterly crushed; I groan in anguish of heart. All my longings lie open before you, O Lord; my sighing is not hidden from you. My heart pounds, my strength fails me; even the light has gone from my eyes" (Ps. 38:8-10).

Hezekiah mourns like a dove: "I cried like a swift or a thrush, I moaned like a mourning dove. My eyes grew weak as I looked at the heavens. I am troubled; O Lord, come to my aid!" (Isa. 38:14). Ephraim moans before the Lord and the Lord hears his cry: " 'I have surely heard Ephraim's moaning,' " God said to his prophet (Jer. 31:18).

In the New Testament, we find the same things. Peter weeps bitterly: "Then Peter remembered the word Jesus had spoken: 'Before the rooster crows, you will disown me three times.' And he went outside and wept bitterly" (Matt. 26:75). Christ had strong cryings and tears in his prayers: "During the days of Jesus' life on earth, he offered up prayers and petitions with loud cries and tears to the one who could save him from death, and he was heard because of his reverent submission" (Heb. 5:7). Christ cried and wept from a sense of the justice of God, the guilt of sin, and the pains of hell and destruction.

We find great solace from the Psalms as they express our inner sensibility in prayer: "I love the LORD, for he heard my voice; he heard my cry for mercy. Because he turned his ear to me, I will call on him as long as I live. The cords of death entangled me, the anguish of the grave came upon me; I was overcome by trouble and sorrow. Then I called on the name of the LORD: 'O LORD, save me!' " (Ps. 116:1-4). In all these instances mentioned here, and in hundreds more that might be named from the

Scriptures, you may see that prayer carries in it a sensible feeling disposition, and often it is awareness of the awfulness of sin.

When in prayer there is a sincere and sensible pouring out of the heart and soul to God, then sometimes there is a sweet sense of receiving mercy—encouraging, comforting, strengthening, enlivening, and enlightening mercy. Thus David pours out his soul to bless and praise and admire the great God for his lovingkindness to such poor sinners. "Praise the LORD, O my soul," he cries, "and forget not all his benefits. He forgives all my sins and heals all my diseases; he redeems my life from the pit and crowns me with love and compassion. He satisfies my desires with good things, so that my youth is renewed like the eagle's" (Ps. 103:2-5).

The prayers of saints are sometimes turned into praise and thanksgiving. God's people pray with their praises, as it is written: "Rejoice in the Lord always. I will say it again: Rejoice! Let your gentleness be evident to all. The Lord is near. Do not be anxious about anything, but in everything, by prayer and petition, with thanksgiving, present your requests to God. And the peace of God, which transcends all understanding, will guard your hearts and your minds in Christ Jesus" (Phil. 4:4-7).

A sensible thanksgiving for mercies received is a mighty prayer in the sight of God. Such a prayer prevails with him unspeakably.

In prayer there is sometimes in the soul a sense of mercy *to be received*. This sets the soul aflame: " 'O LORD Almighty, God of Israel,' " prayed David, " 'you have revealed this to your servant, saying, "I will build a house for you." So your servant has found courage to offer you this prayer. O Sovereign LORD, you are God! Your words are trustworthy, and you have given this good promise to your servant' " (2 Sam. 7:27, 28). Jacob, David, Daniel, and others were given a sense that God wanted to bless them. This prompted them to pray, not by fits and starts, not in a foolish frothy way to babble over a few words written on paper, but mightily, fervently, and continually to groan out their situation before the Lord, as being *sensible* of their needs, their misery, and the willingness of God to show them his mercy.

PRAYER

O Lord, I sometimes moan under the agony of unrepented and unconfessed sin; forgive me for thinking that I could hide my innermost thoughts from you. I do moan when I see the horrible effects which sin has had upon my life and upon the lives of others. I do moan and agonize over the state of this fallen world and over the evil inflicted upon it by the heartless and cruel enemies of your kingdom. I pray for mercy now, and I ask you to assure me by your Word that the victory is indeed already won through faith in Jesus Christ.

Lord, even as I pray, I praise you and thank you for the precious promises of Scripture that I can apply to the needs and groanings of my daily life. I praise you that through the sacrifice you made on the cross, I have received mercy upon mercy both in this life and in the life to come. Use my afflictions, O God, to demonstrate your love and power and wisdom and faithfulness, even to the praise of your glory. Amen.

MEDITATION FOUR
PRAYER INVOLVES THE EMOTIONS

PRAYER is a sincere, sensible, AFFECTIONATE pouring out of the heart or soul to God, through Christ, in the strength and assistance of the Holy Spirit, for such things as God has promised, or according to the Word of God, for the good of the church, with submission in faith to the will of God.

The heat, strength, life, vigor, and *affection* that are in right prayer! "As the deer pants for streams of water, so my soul pants for you, O God" (Ps. 42:1). "How I long for your precepts! Renew my life in your righteousness" (Ps. 119:40). "I long for your salvation, O LORD, and your law is my delight" (Ps. 119:174). "My soul yearns, even faints for the courts of the LORD; my heart and my flesh cry out for the living God" (Ps. 84:2). "My soul is consumed with longing for your laws at all times" (Ps. 119:20). Note that: "My soul is consumed with longing." *Oh, what affection—passion, emotion—there must be in prayer!*

It is similar with Daniel: "O Lord, listen! O Lord, forgive! O Lord, hear and act! For your sake, O my Lord, do not delay, because your city and your people bear your name" (Dan. 9:19). Every syllable carries a mighty intensity and urgency in it. This is called the fervent, or the working

16

prayer, by the Apostle James. And so again it is reported of Jesus, "And being in anguish, he prayed more earnestly, and his sweat was like drops of blood falling to the ground" (Luke 22:44). Jesus had his emotions more and more drawn out after God's helping hand.

But far away from the Bible's example are most people when they pray! Prayer with earnestness and urgency is genuine *prayer* in God's account. Alas, the greatest number of people are not conscious at all of the duty of prayer. And as for those who are, it is to be feared that many of them are very great strangers to sincere, sensible, and *affectionate*—emotional—pouring out of their hearts or souls to God. Too many content themselves with a little lip-service and bodily exercise, mumbling over a few imaginary prayers. When the emotions are involved in such urgency that the soul will waste itself rather than go without the good desired, there is communion and solace with Christ. And hence it is that the saints have spent their strength, and lost their lives, rather than go without the blessings God intended for them.

PRAYER

Dear Father, I love you with my whole heart and being. You have given me life and light in Jesus Christ. You have given me a world where all creation points to you and to your divine character and grace. You have given me the opportunity to join with you and all saints in prayer for the church and for her establishment in every corner of the earth. I long to see you in all of your beauty and excellence, and that longing strengthens me in my pilgrimage. I long for your coming again in power and glory. I long for the redemption of all creation, that is groaning to be released from its bondage to decay. I take delight in the promise that there will be a time when we will see face to face rather than in a mirror dimly. Fill me now with your Holy Spirit as a means not only for loving you perfectly, but to empower me for the tasks I have upon this earth, for Jesus' sake. Amen.

MEDITATION FIVE
POUR OUT YOUR HEART TO GOD

PRAYER is a sincere, sensible, affectionate POURING OUT OF THE HEART OR SOUL TO GOD, through Christ, in the strength and assistance of the Holy Spirit, for such things as God has promised, or according to the Word of God, for the good of the church, with submission in faith to the will of God.

Prayer is a *pouring out of the heart or soul.* There is in prayer an unbosoming of a person's self, an opening of the heart to God, a deeply felt pouring out of the soul in requests, sighs, and groans. "All my longings lie open before you, O Lord, my sighing is not hidden from you," says David (Ps. 38:9). And again, "My soul thirsts for God, for the living God. When can I go and meet with God? These things I remember as I pour out my soul: how I used to go with the multitude, leading the procession to the house of God, with shouts of joy and thanksgiving among the festive throng" (Ps. 42:2, 4). Note that: "I pour out my soul." It is an expression signifying that in prayer you give your whole life and strength to God. And in another place David says, "Trust in him at all times, O people; pour out your hearts to him, for God is our refuge" (Ps. 62:8).

This is the prayer to which the promise is made for the delivering of a poor creature out of captivity: "But if from there you seek the Lord your God, you will find him if you look for him with all your heart and with all your soul" (Deut. 4:29).

Prayer must be a pouring out of the heart or soul *to God*. This shows the excellency of the spirit of prayer. It is the great God of the universe to whom prayer attends.

When shall we come and appear before God? We pray when we see an emptiness in all things under heaven. We see that in God alone there is rest and satisfaction for the soul. "The widow who is really in need and left all alone puts her hope in God and continues night and day to pray and to ask God for help" (1 Tim. 5:5). So says David, "In you, O LORD, I have taken refuge; let me never be put to shame. Rescue me and deliver me in your righteousness; turn your ear to me and save me. Be my rock of refuge, to which I can always go; give the command to save me, for you are my rock and my fortress. Deliver me, O my God, from the hand of the wicked, from the grasp of evil and cruel men. For you have been my hope, O Sovereign LORD, my confidence since my youth" (Ps. 71:1-5).

To pray rightly, you must make God your hope, stay, and all. Right prayer sees nothing substantial or worth being concerned about except God. And that, as I said before, it does in a *sincere*, *sensible*, and *affectionate* way.

PRAYER

O Lord, my enemies are encamped all about me, even my spiritual foes. They would have me sink again into the miry clay of sin and defeat. They would entice me to sin once again, or they would drive others to sin against me. Protect me, O my God; send forth your ministering angels to meet my needs. May they build a hedge about me so the darts of the evil one will not reach my heart. O Lord, I give my whole self to you. To whom can I turn if not to you? You are my strength and my Redeemer. I trust in you and I will not fear, for you are on your throne and I am ever before you through the blood of Jesus Christ. It is through him that I offer my prayers to you, O God. Amen.

MEDITATION SIX
PRAYER THROUGH CHRIST

PRAYER is a sincere, sensible, affectionate pouring out of the heart or soul to God, THROUGH CHRIST, in the strength and assistance of the Holy Spirit, for such things as God has promised, or according to the Word, for the good of the church, with submission in faith to the will of God.

This *through Christ* must be added or else we might question whether or not it is true prayer, even though in appearance it may be eloquent.

Christ is the way through whom the soul gains admittance to God, and without Christ it is impossible that what you desire should come into the care of the Lord. Scripture teaches, "Jesus answered, 'I am the way and the truth and the life. No one comes to the Father except through me' " (John 14:6). And further, let it be noted that Jesus also said, " 'And I will do whatever you ask in my name, so that the Son may bring glory to the Father. You may ask me for anything in my name, and I will do it' " (John 14:13, 14).

This was Daniel's way in praying for the people of God. He did it in the name of Christ: " 'Now, our God, hear the prayers and petitions of your servant. For your sake, O Lord, look with favor on your desolate sanctuary' "

(Dan. 9:17). And so David: "For the sake of your name, O Lord," that is, for Christ's sake, "forgive my iniquity, though it is great" (Ps. 25:11).

Not everyone who makes mention of Christ's name in prayer effectively prays to God in the name of Christ, or through him. Coming to God *through Christ* is the hardest part that is found in prayer. A person may more easily be sensible of Christ's works, and sincerely desire his mercy, and yet not be able to come to God through Christ. The person who comes to God through Christ must first have the knowledge of him: "And without faith it is impossible to please God, because anyone who comes to him must believe that he exists and that he rewards those who earnestly seek him" (Heb. 11:6). And so he who comes to God through Christ must be enabled to know Christ. Moses says " 'Teach me your ways so I may know you and continue to find favor with you' " (Exod. 33:13).

No one but the Father can truly reveal Jesus Christ: " 'All things have been committed to me by my Father. No one knows the Son except the Father, and no one knows the Father except the Son and those to whom the Son chooses to reveal him' " (Matt. 11:27). To come to God through Christ means God has placed you under the shadow of the Lord Jesus, as a person is sheltered under a thing for safeguard. This is why David so often refers to the Lord as his shield, buckler, tower, fortress, and rock of defense (Pss. 18, 27, and 28), not only because he overcame his enemies by Christ, but because through Christ he found favor with God the Father.

And so God said to Abraham: "After this, the word of the Lord came to Abram in a vision: 'Do not be afraid, Abram. I am your shield, your very great reward' " (Gen. 15:1). The person then who comes to God through Christ must have faith, by which he puts his trust in Christ, so that he appears before God in Christ.

He who has faith is born of God, born again, and so becomes one of the sons of God. As a son of God, he is joined to Christ and made a member of him. "Jesus answered, 'I tell you the truth, no one can enter the kingdom of God unless he is born of water and the Spirit. Flesh gives birth to flesh, but the Spirit gives birth to spirit' " (John 3:5, 6). And therefore, you who are born again, you can as a member of Christ come to God. I say, *as a member of Christ*, for God looks on the Christian as a part of Christ, part of his body, united to him by election, conversion, illumination, the Spirit being conveyed into the heart by God, "for we are members of his body" (Eph. 5:30).

So now we can come to God in Christ's merits, in his blood, righteousness, victory, intercession, and so stand before God, being accepted because we are united with the one he loves. You are a member of the Lord Jesus Christ, and under this consideration have admittance to come before God. By virtue of your union with Christ, the Holy Spirit is given to abide in you. For this reason, you are able to pour out yourself before God in prayer, with his attention to your case and with the willingness to answer.

PRAYER

O Lord, I give you thanks that in all my prayers I do come to you through Jesus Christ, because his blood shed for my sins covers me and enables me to approach the throne of grace. May I more consciously recognize my need of Jesus in all that I do, and especially in my prayers. May I honor him more as I seek to bring glory to you in all my requests. Teach me to pray for

*those things which will be for the good of your church. Inspire
me by your Holy Spirit to pray for those people and things
you would have me pray for in the faith that you would hear
me and want to answer my prayer through Jesus' name and
for his sake. Amen.*

MEDITATION SEVEN
PRAYER IN THE HOLY SPIRIT

PRAYER is a sincere, sensible, affectionate pouring out of the heart or soul to God, through Christ, IN THE STRENGTH AND ASSISTANCE OF THE HOLY SPIRIT, for such things as God has promised, or according to the Word of God, for the good of the church, with submission in faith to the will of God.

Praying through Christ, praying in union with Christ, and praying in the strength and assistance of the Holy Spirit depend so much upon one another that it is impossible for prayer to be prayer apart from this relationship. Though some prayers be ever so eloquent, apart from Christ and the Holy Spirit the prayers are rejected by God. For without a sincere, sensible, affectionate pouring out of the heart to God, prayer is but lip-labor. If your prayers are not through Christ, they fall far short of ever sounding well in the ears of God. So also, if your prayers are not in the strength and assistance of the Holy Spirit, you are like the sons of Aaron, offering with strange fire: "Aaron's sons Nadab and Abihu took their censers, put fire in them and added incense; and they offered unauthorized fire before the LORD, contrary to his command. So fire came out from the presence of the LORD and consumed them, and they died before the LORD. Moses then said to Aaron, 'This is what the LORD spoke of when he said: "Among those who approach me I will show myself holy; in the sight of all the people I will be honored." ' Aaron remained silent" (Lev. 10:1-3). But I shall speak more of this later. In the meantime, let it be remembered that whatever is *not* petitioned through the teaching and assistance of the Holy Spirit cannot possibly be according to the will of God. As Paul wrote to the Romans, "In the same way, the Spirit helps us in our weakness. We do not know what we ought to pray, but the Spirit himself intercedes for us with groans that words cannot express. And he who searches our hearts knows the mind of the Spirit, because the Spirit intercedes for the saints in accordance with God's will" (Rom. 8:26, 27). No man nor church in the world can come to God in prayer except by the assistance of the Holy Spirit. "For through him we both have access to the Father by one Spirit" (Eph. 2:18). Because there is in these Scriptures so full a revelation of the spirit of prayer, and of man's inability to pray without the Holy Spirit's aid; therefore, I shall in a few words comment upon it.

"We do not know what we ought to pray, . . ."

Consider the person speaking, the Apostle Paul himself. In effect Paul is saying, "We apostles, we extraordinary officers, we wise master builders, some of whom have been caught up into paradise—*we* do not know what we should pray for, apart from the Holy Spirit's assistance." (See also Rom. 15:16; 1 Cor. 3:10; 2 Cor. 12:4.) Surely no man will claim that Paul and the other apostles were not as able to have done any work for God as any pope or church official. The apostles could have written a *Book of Common Prayer* as well as those who at first composed it. They were not lacking in either grace or gifts. But they chose not to write a prayer book.* Yet the supposedly wise men of our days think they are so well skilled that they have both the form and the substance of prayer at their fingertips. They set a certain prayer for each day—years before it comes! There is a prayer for Christmas, another for Easter, and others for the six days after that. The church officials have also determined how many syllables must be said in every one of their prayers at public worship. For each saint's day also, they have prayers ready for the generations yet unborn to say. The authors of the *Book of Common Prayer* chose to do what the apostles would not do: establish certain prayers to be used again and again. The apostles did not do so because, as Paul admitted, "we do not know what we ought to pray"—unless the Spirit intercedes.

"We do not know what we ought to pray." We know not the matter of the things for which we should pray, neither the objects for which we are to pray, nor the medium by or through whom we pray. We know none of these things except by the assistance of the Spirit. Should we pray for communion with God through Christ? Should we pray for faith, for justification by grace, and a truly sanctified heart? We know none of these things unless the Spirit prompts us to pray for them. "For who among men knows the thoughts of a man except the man's spirit within him? In the same way no one knows the thoughts of God except the Spirit of God" (1 Cor. 2:11). The Apostle speaks of inward and spiritual things which the world knows not.

---

*Bunyan was in prison at this time for preaching and praying his own prayers in public. He was writing and fighting for the right of people to pray prayers other than those prepared and printed in the Church of England's *Book of Common Prayer*. He was determined to teach those who knew no other method of prayer what Scripture teaches about how they could pray their own prayers to God.

PRAYER

Dear Father, in the name of Jesus Christ, I pray that you will send your Holy Spirit down upon me. Anoint me, fill me, use me, teach me how to pray as I ought. Dear Father, in my own strength I am less than useless. Empower me, as I strive to obey you and do the tasks you have assigned me this day. Motivate me to pray beyond any written prayer to really express my deepest longings and need of you. I praise you for the Holy Spirit when he reveals any unconfessed sins that are blocking my path to deeper communion with you. I thank you for my Savior Jesus Christ, who is ready and willing to intercede for me. Help me to love much, and be gracious to all those who need my care, concern, and compassion through Jesus Christ. Amen.

MEDITATION EIGHT
PRAYER AND THE WORD OF GOD

PRAYER is a sincere, sensible, affectionate pouring out of the heart or soul to God, through Christ, in the strength and assistance of the Holy Spirit, FOR SUCH THINGS AS GOD HAS PROMISED, OR ACCORDING TO THE WORD, for the good of the church, with submission in faith to the will of God.

Jesus commanded, "When you pray, go into your room, close the door and pray to your Father, who is unseen. Then your Father, who sees what is done in secret, will reward you. And when you pray, do not keep on babbling like pagans, for they think they will be heard because of their many words. Do not be like them, for your Father knows what you need before you ask him" (Matt. 6:6-8). It is prayer when it is within the compass of God's Word; and it is blasphemy, or at best vain babbling, when the petition is contrary to the Book. David, therefore, while in prayer, kept his eye on the Word of God: "I am laid low in the dust; renew my life according to your word. . . . My soul is weary with sorrow; strengthen me according to your word" (Ps. 119:25, 28). And indeed, the Holy Spirit does not immediately enliven the heart of the praying

Christian without the Word, but only by, with, and through the Word. The Holy Spirit brings the Word to the heart, and opens the Word to us so that we are provoked to go to the Lord in prayer and tell him how it is with us. We also are led to argue and plead according to the Word.

This was the experience of Daniel, that mighty prophet of God. Daniel, understanding that the captivity of the children of Israel was near to an end, made his prayer to God. "In the first year of Darius son of Xerxes (a Mede by descent), who was made ruler over the Babylonian kingdom—in the first year of his reign, I, Daniel, understood from the Scriptures, according to the Word of the LORD given to Jeremiah the prophet, that the desolation of Jerusalem would last seventy years. So I turned to the Lord God and pleaded with him in prayer and petition, in fasting, and in sackcloth and ashes" (Dan. 9:1-3). So I say, as the Spirit is the helper and the governor of the soul, when you pray according to the will of God, you should be guided by and pray according to the Word of God and his promises.

Hence, our Lord Jesus Christ did come to a stop in his prayer for deliverance, although his life lay at stake for it. He said that he could pray to his Father, and that the Father could give him twelve legions of angels; but how then would the Scriptures be fulfilled (see Matt. 26:53, 54)? Were there but a word for it in the Scriptures, then Jesus would have soon been out of the hands of his enemies and would have soon been helped by the angels. But the Scriptures would not warrant this type of praying because they had indicated that he was to die for our sins. True prayer, then, must be according to the Word of God and his promises. The Spirit by the Word must direct both the manner and the matter of prayer. "So what shall I do?" asks Paul, "I will pray with my spirit, but I will also pray with my mind; I will sing with my spirit, but I will also sing with my mind" (1 Cor. 14:15).* There is no understanding without the Word. For if people reject the Word of God, "what kind of wisdom do they have?" (Jer. 8:9).

PRAYER

Dear heavenly Father, even as Paul desired to speak sound words in prayer by the Holy Spirit's leading, so I pray that you would reveal to me the promises and words of Scripture that I may claim for my particular situations in life. I pray that you would guide me in the application of your Word in prayer, so that I might pray in accordance with your will and then be able to manifest your glorious loving power to all for Jesus' sake. Amen.

---

*Bunyan and many other Bible expositors have translated and interpreted this verse to read, "I will pray with the Spirit, but I will also pray with my mind." It is in this sense that Bunyan uses this verse in the context here.

38

MEDITATION NINE
PRAYER FOR
THE CHURCH

PRAYER is a sincere, sensible, affectionate pouring out of the heart or soul to God, through Christ, in the strength and assistance of the Holy Spirit, for such things as God has promised, or according to the Word, FOR THE GOOD OF THE CHURCH, with submission in faith to the will of God.

This clause, *for the good of the church,* includes whatever brings honor to God, Christ, or his people. For God and Christ and the church are so linked together that if the good of one is prayed for, then the church, the glory of God, and the advancement of Christ must all be included. For as Christ is in the Father, so the saints are in Christ. When you pray for other Christians, you touch the apple of God's eye. Therefore, if you pray for the peace of Jerusalem (that is, for the church), then you pray for all that is required of you. For the church will never be in perfect peace until she is in heaven; and there is nothing that Christ more desires than to have her there. That also is the place that God through Christ has given her. The Christian who prays for the peace and good of Jerusalem, the church, asks in prayer for that which Christ has purchased with his blood; and also that which the Father has given to him as the price thereof.

Now he who prays for this must pray for abundance of grace for the church and for help against all her temptations; that God would let nothing be too hard for her; that all things might work together for her good; and that God would keep her blameless. The Scriptures have taught us to pray "To him who is able to keep you from falling and to present you before his glorious presence without fault and with great joy—to the only God our Savior be glory, majesty, power and authority, through Jesus Christ our Lord, before all ages, now and forevermore! Amen" (Jude 24, 25).

We should pray for God to protect and defend his sons to his glory, in the midst of a crooked and perverse nation. This must be our daily prayer. And this is the substance of Christ's own prayer in the seventeenth chapter of John. All of Paul's prayers ran in the same way, as one of his prayers eminently shows: "And this is my prayer: that your love may abound more and more in knowledge and depth of insight, so that you may be able to discern what is best and may be pure and blameless until the day of Christ, filled with the fruit of righteousness that comes through Jesus Christ—to the glory and praise of God" (Phil. 1:9-11). Paul's prayer was a short prayer, you see, and yet full of good desires for the church, from the beginning to the end. He prayed that she might go on in the most excellent frame of spirit, without blame, sincere, and without offense, until the day of Christ, let her temptations or persecutions be what they will. See especially Paul's own prayers and account of his prayers in Ephesians 1:16-20; 3:14-19; and Colossians 1:9-13.

PRAYER

Dear heavenly Father, I confess that many of my prayers are truly selfish, because I neglect to pray for the good of your church and the welfare of your servants around the world. I thank you for the great honor that you have bestowed upon all Christians, by making our prayers count for the good of your church and for the sanctification of believers. Please continue to inspire us by your Spirit and your Word so that we might know your will for the church so, like Daniel praying for the return of the Israelites to Jerusalem, we might pray for those things you intend for your church on earth. In the name of your Son, Jesus Christ, I pray these things. Amen.

MEDITATION TEN
PRAYING IN THE WILL OF GOD

PRAYER is a sincere, sensible, affectionate pouring out of the heart or soul to God, through Christ, in the strength and assistance of the Holy Spirit, for such things as God has promised, or according to the Word, for the good of the church, WITH SUBMISSION IN FAITH TO THE WILL OF GOD.

True prayer submits to the will of God and says, "your will be done" (Matt. 6:10). Therefore, the people of the Lord in humility are to lay themselves and their prayers, and all that they have, at the foot of their God to be disposed of by him as he in his heavenly wisdom sees best. Yet when we lay our whole selves before him, we do not doubt but that God will answer our prayers in a way that shall be most for our advantage *and* his glory. When the saints of God, therefore, pray with submission to the will of God, they do not argue or doubt or question but trust *in faith* God's love and kindness to them. They recognize that they are not at all times wise, and that sometimes Satan may get the advantage over them, so to tempt them to pray for that which, if they had it, would prove to be for neither God's glory nor his people's best interest and good.

John wrote in his letter, "This is the confidence we have in approaching God: that if we ask anything according to his will, he hears us. And if we know that he hears us— whatever we ask—we know that we have what we asked of him" (1 John 5:14, 15). For as I have said before, the petition that is not brought before God in and through the Holy Spirit will not be answered, because it is outside the will of God. For only the Holy Spirit knows how to pray according to the will of God. "However, as it is written: 'No eye has seen, no ear has heard, no mind has conceived what God has prepared for those who love him'—but God has revealed it to us by his Spirit. The Spirit searches all things, even the deep things of God. For who among men knows the thoughts of a man except the man's spirit within him? In the same way no one knows the thoughts of God except the Spirit of God" (1 Cor. 2:9-11). And likewise, "We do not know what we ought to pray for" (Rom. 8:26).

Note this: *"what we ought to pray for"*! If we do not think about this, or if we do not understand its meaning in the spirit and the truth of it, we may devise, as King Jeroboam did, a way of worship different from what is revealed in the Word of God. "Jeroboam thought to himself, 'The kingdom will now likely revert to the house of David. If these people go up to offer sacrifices at the temple of the LORD in Jerusalem, they will again give their allegiance to their lord, Rehoboam king of Judah. They will kill me and return to King Rehoboam.' After seeking advice, the king made two golden calves. He said to the people, 'It is too much for you to go up to Jerusalem. Here are your gods, O Israel, who brought you up out of Egypt.' One he set up at Bethel, and the other in Dan. And this thing became sin; the people went even as far as Dan to worship the one there" (1 Kings 12:26-30). Jeroboam's shrines, built contrary to God's will, are condemned many times throughout the Old Testament.

Paul says that we must pray as we ought; and this we ourselves cannot do by all the art, skill, and cunning devices of men or angels. "We do not know what we ought to pray for, but the Spirit himself"; indeed, *it must be the Spirit himself* who helps us in our infirmities, not the Spirit combined with our lusts. What man of his own brain may imagine and devise is one thing, and what we are commanded and ought to do is another. Many ask and do not receive because they ask amiss, and so are never any nearer enjoying those things they ask for: "When you ask, you do not receive, because you ask with wrong motives, that you may spend what you get on your pleasures" (James 4:3).

Praying your own prayers apart from a prayer book will not put off God. But neither will it cause him to answer your prayer. While you are praying, God is searching your heart to see from what root and spirit your prayer arises. "This is the assurance we have in approaching God": wrote John, "that if we ask anything *according to his will*, he hears us" (1 John 5:14). And again Paul wrote, "And he who searches our hearts knows the mind of the Spirit, because the Spirit intercedes for the saints *in accordance with God's will*" (Rom. 8:27). For only what is according to his will does he hear, and nothing else. Only the Holy Spirit can teach us to pray according to God's will. Only the Spirit can search out all things, even the deep things of God. Without the Holy Spirit, we would not know what we ought to pray for, especially since we have infirmities which make us absolutely incapable of praying *according to God's will*.

PRAYER

Come Holy Spirit, dwell in my heart and soul and mind and spirit. Reveal to me the things of God's mind and will that I might pray according to what he has planned for me and for his church. Guide me as I read the Scriptures that I might see the promises God has for me and for his church, and teach me to pray and claim these promises in his behalf. Forgive me for my little faith, which too often fails to trust that you really are working in my best interests and good through Jesus Christ. Amen.

MEDITATION ELEVEN
THE SPIRIT OVERCOMES OUR WEAKNESSES

WITHOUT the Holy Spirit, we are so weak that we cannot by any other means be enabled to think one right saving thought of God, of Christ, or of the blessings he has reserved for those who love him. Therefore, the psalmist said of the wicked, "In his pride the wicked does not seek him; in all his thoughts there is no room for God" (Ps. 10:4). The wicked might imagine God as a being such as they are themselves. Prior to the great flood, God looked upon the earth and, "The LORD saw how great man's wickedness on the earth had become, and that every inclination of the thoughts of his heart was only evil all the time" (Gen. 6:5). And after the flood, when Noah sacrificed to God, "The LORD smelled the pleasing aroma and said in his heart: 'Never again will I curse the ground because of man, even though every inclination of his heart is evil from childhood' " (Gen. 8:21). Since men are not able to conceive rightly of God to whom they pray, of Christ through whom they pray, nor of the things for which they pray, how shall they be able to address themselves to God, unless the Spirit helps in this weakness?

The Holy Spirit is the revealer of things to us poor souls

and he gives us understanding of them; therefore, Christ told his disciples, when he promised to send the Holy Spirit, the Comforter, "He will bring glory to me by taking from what is mine and making it known to you" (John 16:14). It is as if Christ had said, "I know you are naturally dark and ignorant as to understanding any of my things. Though you try this course and the other, yet your ignorance will still remain, as if a veil is spread over your heart. And there is no one who can take away that veil or give you spiritual understanding except the Holy Spirit."

Right prayer must, both in the outward expression and in the inward intention, come from what the soul apprehends in the light of the Holy Spirit. Otherwise it is condemned as vain and an abomination, because the heart and tongue do not go along jointly in the same intention, neither indeed can they unless the Spirit helps our infirmities and weaknesses. And this David knew full well when he cried, "O Lord, open my lips, and my mouth will declare your praise" (Ps. 51:15). I suppose that most can imagine that David could speak and express himself as well as others, as well as any in our generation, as is clearly manifested by his words and by his works. Nevertheless when this good and eloquent man went into God's worship, the Lord had to help him or he could have done nothing: "O Lord, open my lips, and my mouth will declare your praise." He could not speak one right word unless the Holy Spirit gave him proper utterance. "The Spirit helps us in our weakness. We do not know what we ought to pray, but the Spirit himself intercedes for us with groans that words cannot express" (Rom. 8:26).

PRAYER

O Lord God, I thank you for the blessing of your Word and your Spirit, for by your Word I can know many of the deep things of you, and by your Spirit I can understand and apply these deep things to my life and in my conversations with others. Only too well do I recognize my weakness and my inability to know or do any good thing apart from you, and I thank you for your Spirit who is an ever present help in any time of weakness or trouble. Please continue to lead me in the paths of righteousness for your name's sake. Amen.

MEDITATION TWELVE
THE SPIRIT AND
EFFECTIVE PRAYER

EFFECTIVE praying must be praying with the Holy Spirit, because without the Spirit we are senseless, hypocritical, cold, and improper in our prayers. Without the assistance of the Holy Spirit, our prayers are abominable to God: "Woe to you, teachers of the law and Pharisees, you hypocrites! You devour widows' houses and for a show make lengthy prayers. Therefore you will be punished more severely" (Matt. 23:14). God does not regard the excellency of the voice, nor the seeming earnestness and fervor of the person praying, unless the Holy Spirit is aiding the person in his prayer. Man by himself is so full of all manner of wickedness, that he cannot make a word or a thought or prayer clean and acceptable to God; he must have the guidance of the Holy Spirit. For this reason, the Pharisees, with all their fine prayers, were rejected. The Pharisees were excellently able to express themselves in words, and also for length of time spent in prayer they were very notable. But they had not the Spirit to help them, so they did what they did with their infirmities and weaknesses only. They fell far short of a sincere, sensible, affectionate pouring out of their souls to God, through the strength of the Holy Spirit. The prayer that ascends to heaven is the prayer that is sent there by the Holy Spirit, and it is that prayer which is effective.

Nothing but the Spirit can show a man clearly his misery by nature and put him into a posture of prayer. Talk is but talk and so our prayers are only mouth-worship if there is not a sense of misery in sin. O the cursed hypocrisy that is in most hearts and that accompanies many thousands of praying men! But the Spirit will show the soul its misery, where it is in its spiritual growth, and what is likely to become of it apart from Christ, and also the intolerableness of its condition apart from faith in the Savior. For it is the Spirit who effectively convinces of sin and misery without the Lord Jesus, and so puts the soul into a sweet, serious, sensible, affectionate way of praying to God according to his Word: "But I tell you the truth: It is for your good that I am going away. Unless I go away, the Counselor will not come to you; but if I go, I will send him to you. When he comes, he will convict the world of guilt in regard to sin and righteousness and judgment: in regard to sin, because men do not believe in me; in regard to righteousness, because I am going to the Father, where you can see me no longer; and in regard to judgment, because the prince of this world now stands condemned" (John 16:7-11).

Even if men did see their sins, without the help of the Holy Spirit they *would* not pray. Instead, they would run away from God and utterly despair of mercy. Such were the cases of Adam and Eve, Cain, and Judas. When a man is indeed in despair over his sin and God's curse, then it is a difficult thing to persuade him to pray. Apart from the influence of the Holy Spirit a sinner will say, " 'It's no use. We will continue with our own plans; each of us will follow the stubbornness of his evil heart' " (Jer. 18:12). A sinner has often concluded, "I am so low, so wretched, and so cursed a creature, that I shall never be regarded by God!" Now here comes the Spirit, who calms the soul and helps the soul hold up its face to God by letting into the heart some small sense of mercy to encourage it to go to God. This is why the Spirit is called "the Comforter."

PRAYER

Dear heavenly Father, forgive me for being so blind to your work in my life. I confess that I have not glorified you, and I have not recognized fully the wonderful work of your Spirit in my life. Forgive me for not acknowledging you to be the loving and gracious God that you are, and for failing to thank you for leading me out of the darkness and into the light by your Spirit, even when I was inclined to live my own life without regard to you or your concerns. May I now seek to honor you by sharing with others the good news of how you work in our lives, even while we are yet sinners, that we might learn to pray through the Holy Spirit. Amen.

MEDITATION THIRTEEN
THE RIGHT WAY TO PRAY

NO ONE can know how to come to God the right way unless he learns how to pray in or with the Holy Spirit. People may easily say that they come to God in his Son, but it is the hardest thing for anyone to come to God the right way and in his own way without the Spirit.

The Spirit must show us the way of coming to God, and also what there is in God that makes him desirable. "If I have found favor in your eyes," prayed Moses, "teach me your ways so I may know you and continue to find favor with you" (Exod. 33:13). And Jesus taught about the Spirit, "He will bring glory to me by taking from what is mine and making it known to you" (John 16:14).

Without the Holy Spirit, though you might see your misery and sin, and also the way to come to God, yet you would never be able to claim a share in either God, Christ, or mercy. O how great a task it is for a poor soul that becomes aware of its sin and the wrath of God to say in faith but this one word, "Father." I tell you the difficulty is in this very thing: the soul aware of its sin is afraid to call God, "Father." "Oh!" says the sinner, "I dare not call him, 'Father.' " Therefore the Holy Spirit must be sent into the hearts of God's people for this very thing, to help us cry "Father." It is too great a thing and too great a work for any man to knowingly and believingly call God "Father" without the Holy Spirit's aid. "Because you are sons, God sent the Spirit of his Son into our hearts, the Spirit who calls out, 'Abba, Father' " (Gal. 4:6). When I say *knowingly* I mean knowing what it is to be a child of God and to be born again. And when I say *believingly* I mean, the soul believes, from good experience, that the work of grace is wrought in him. This is the right way to call upon God, "Father." And not everyone who prays the *Lord's Prayer* from memory truly regards God as his Father. No, here is the life of prayer, when in or with the Spirit, a person being made sensible of his sin, and of how to come to the Lord for mercy, comes and says in the strength of the Spirit, "Father." That one word spoken *in faith* is better than a thousand prayers, written or read, in a formal, cold, mechanical way.

How far short are those people who count it enough to teach themselves and their children to say the *Lord's Prayer*, the creed, and the other sayings. God knows they are unaware of themselves, their misery in sin, or of what it is to be brought to God through Christ! Ah, poor soul! Study your misery! Cry to God to show you your confused blindness and ignorance, before you be so bold in calling God your Father or teaching your children to do so. And know that to say God is your Father in prayer or conversation, without any experience of the work of grace in your souls, is to say you are a *Christian* when you are not, and so you lie! You say, "Our Father," and God says, "You blaspheme!" You say that you are true Christians, but God says, "You lie!" Our risen Lord told the church in Smyrna: "These are the words of him who is the First and the Last, who died and came to life again. I know your afflictions and your poverty—yet you are rich! I know the slander of those who say they are Jews and are not, but are a synagogue of Satan" (Rev. 2:8, 9). And he told the church in Philadelphia: "I will make those who are of the synagogue of Satan, who claim to be Jews though they are not, but are liars—I will make them come and fall down at your feet and acknowledge that I have loved you" (Rev. 3:9). And so much the greater is the sin when the sinner boasts his pretended sanctity, as the Jews did to Christ in the eighth chapter of the Gospel of John. Their boasting made Christ tell them in plain terms their doom for all their hypocritical pretenses:

> "Abraham is our father," they answered.
>
> "If you were Abraham's children," said Jesus, "then you would do the things Abraham did. As it is, you are determined to kill me, a man who has told you the truth that I heard from God. Abraham did not do such things. You are doing the things your own father does."
>
> "We are not illegitimate children," they protested. "The only Father we have is God himself."
>
> Jesus said to them, "If God were your Father, you would love me, for I came from God and now am here. I have not come on my own; but he sent me. Why is my language not clear to you? Because you are unable to hear what I say. You belong to your father, the devil, and you want to carry out your father's desire. He was a murderer from the beginning, not holding to the truth, for there is no truth in him. When he lies, he speaks his native language, for he is a liar and the father of lies. Yet because I tell the truth, you do not believe me! Can any of you prove me guilty of sin? If I am telling the truth, why don't you believe me? He who belongs to God hears what God says. The reason you do not hear is that you do not belong to God" (John 8:39-47).

Come to know God personally as your Father by putting your faith and trust in his Son. Pray to God as your Father, and ask him to fill your heart with his loving presence.

PRAYER

O Father, forgive me for all the times I have taken for granted the blessed opportunity to call you "Abba." Since I have been adopted by you through faith in your Son Jesus Christ as my Lord and Savior, you have given me the privilege of coming to you as your little child. But I confess that I have sometimes come to you childishly without counting my blessings and also the great price you paid so I could call you, "Father." Please continue to bestow upon me the workings of your grace for Jesus' sake. Amen.

MEDITATION FOURTEEN
PRAYING THE LORD'S PRAYER

PERHAPS your favorite prayer is the *Lord's Prayer:* "Our Father in heaven . . ." (Matt. 6:9). Do you know the *meaning* of the very first words of this prayer? Can you indeed, with the rest of the saints, cry "Our Father"? Are you truly born again? Have you received the Spirit of adoption? Do you see yourself *in Christ,* and can you come to God as a member in him? Or are you ignorant of these things, but still dare to say "Our Father"? Is the Devil really your father? Are you a desperate persecutor of the children of God? Have you cursed them in your heart many a time? Just because the saints were commanded to pray "Our Father," all the blind, ignorant, sinful rabble in the world feel they must use the same words, "Our Father." People who attend church only because they have been taught to do so by their parents—these people call God "Father," though they may have had no personal experience of God as Father.

Do you pray "Hallowed be your name" with all your heart? Do you study, by all honest and lawful ways, to advance the name, holiness, and majesty of God? Do your heart and conversation agree with these words? Do you strive to imitate Christ in all the works of righteousness which God commands you and prompts you to do? It is so if you are one who can truly cry with God's permission "Our Father."

Or is the imitation of Christ one of the least of your thoughts all the day, so that you are actually a hypocrite? Would you have the kingdom of God come indeed, and also his will to be done on earth as it is in heaven? Or would the sound of his trumpet make you run mad, afraid to see the rising of the dead, and afraid to reckon for all of the deeds you have done in the body? Are all the thoughts of it altogether displeasing to you? If God's will were to be done on the earth, would it be to your ruin? There is never in heaven a rebel against God. If a man is a rebel on earth, must he not whirl down to hell? How sad would those men look, and with what terror would they walk up and down the world, if they knew the lying and blaspheming that proceed out of their mouths even in their most pretended sanctity! May the Lord awaken you and teach you poor souls, in all humility, to take heed lest you be rash and unadvised with your heart, and much more with your mouth!

When you appear before God, as the wise man said, "Do not be quick with your mouth, do not be hasty in your heart to utter anything before God. God is in heaven and you are on earth, so let your words be few" (Eccles. 5:2). Especially so, when you call God "Father" without some blessed experience and assurance of being born again.

PRAYER

O Father! I know that I have repeated the Lord's Prayer perhaps thousands of times without any real thought of what I was praying. I am conscious that I am a Christian, a born-again believer, who has every right to call you "Father," but I am aware and I confess that I have taken this privilege too lightly. I confess that there have been many times when, if your will had been done and your kingdom come, as I had prayed, that many of my plans and ways of living would have been radically disrupted. Help me in the future, as your Spirit guides me and prompts me, to really pray the Lord's Prayer from my heart. Lead me to pray expectantly and anxiously for that prayer to be answered in my life now as well as when you come again. Through the name of your Son, Jesus, I offer this prayer. Amen.

MEDITATION FIFTEEN
LIFT UP YOUR HEART TO GOD

TRUE prayer must be praying with the Holy Spirit, if it be accepted by God, because there is nothing but the Spirit who can lift up the heart to God in prayer: "To man belong the plans of the heart, but from the LORD comes the reply of the tongue. All a man's ways seem innocent to him, but motives are weighed by the Lord. Commit to the LORD whatever you do, and your plans will succeed" (Prov. 16:1-3). That is, in every work for God, and especially in prayer, if the heart runs with the tongue it must be prepared by the Spirit of God. Indeed the tongue is very apt, of itself, to run without either fear or wisdom: but when the tongue speaks the answer of the heart, a heart prepared by the Holy Spirit, then the tongue speaks as God commands and desires.

They are mighty words of David, where he said that he lifted his heart and soul to God: "To you, O LORD, I lift up my soul; in you I trust, O my God" (Ps. 25:1). It is a great work for any man without the strength of the Spirit to lift his heart and soul to God; therefore, I conceive that this is one of the great reasons why the Spirit of God is called the Spirit of supplication: "And I will pour out on the house of David and the inhabitants of Jerusalem a spirit of grace and supplication" (Zech. 12:10). The Holy Spirit helps the heart when it makes its supplication, its plea; therefore, wrote Paul, "And pray in the Spirit on all occasions with all kinds of prayers and requests" (Eph. 6:18). And so also in the text we have been considering, "I will pray with the Spirit." Without your heart in it, prayer is like a sound without a life. And a heart will never pray to God unless it is lifted up by the Holy Spirit.

PRAYER

I thank you, Father, for the gift of your Holy Spirit, for the gift of the Scriptures, and for the gift of grace to your servants, such as John Bunyan, so that your will might be opened to me and to many others as well. I praise you for shining your revealing light upon Bunyan while he was in the dark confines of his prison cell. I thank you for opening up to him the many Scriptures he has used in his studies of prayer and the Christian life. And I praise you and thank you further that even though Bunyan has passed from this world to the next, still he speaks! Inspire me, I pray, so I might do for others what you have done for me through others. In Jesus' name. Amen.

MEDITATION SIXTEEN
HOW TO REST IN GOD

AS your heart must be lifted up by the Holy Spirit if you are to pray rightly, so also your heart must be held up by the Holy Spirit when it is up, if you are to continue to pray rightly. I do not know how it is with others' hearts, whether they be lifted up by the Spirit of God and continued so or not, but there are some things I am sure of.

I know it is impossible that all the prayer books and written prayers that men have made in the world should by themselves lift up or prepare the heart to pray to God: that is the work of our great God himself. And I am sure that the prayer books are far from able to keep men's hearts up when they are up. And indeed here is the life of prayer, to have your heart kept with God in the duty of prayer.

The lack of keeping your heart at rest with God in prayer is what God complains of. Men draw nigh to him with their mouths, and honor him with their lips, but their hearts are far from him. "The Lord says: 'These people come near to me with their mouth and honor me with their lips, but their hearts are far from me. Their worship of me is made up only of rules taught by men' " (Isa. 29:13). In Matthew 15:7-9, Jesus called the people who pray in such a way "hypocrites."

May I speak of my own experience, and tell you the difficulty of praying to God as I ought? When I go to pray, I find my heart is disinclined to go to God; and when it is with him, it is disinclined to stay with him. Many times I am forced in my prayers to beg God to take my heart and set it upon himself in Christ. And I beg that, when it is there, he would keep it there. Many times I know not what to pray for, I am so blind. At times I know not how to pray, I am so ignorant. But the Spirit helps us in our weakness: "Teach me your way, O LORD, and I will walk in your truth; give me an undivided heart, that I may fear your name. I will praise you, O Lord my God, with all my heart; I will glorify your name forever" (Ps. 86:11, 12).

The difficulties that the heart has in the time of prayer! No one knows how many byways and back lanes the heart has in which to slip away from the presence of God. How much pride the heart has, if enabled with expressive language to pray to him! How much hypocrisy, if praying before others! And how little consciousness is there of prayer between God and the soul in secret, unless the Spirit of supplication is there to help! When the Holy Spirit gets into the heart, then there is prayer indeed, and not until then.

PRAYER

O Lord God, I am learning that I can do nothing apart from your Holy Spirit. Your Spirit lifts me up in prayer. Your Spirit prepares my heart for prayer. Your Spirit aids me in resting my heart and mind in you in prayer. Your Spirit prompts me to pray for the things of your heart, and he leads me beyond selfish desires. May I be continually inspired by your Spirit to say and do and pray consistently, that my life might be a witness to others regarding the blessed power of prayer and your work through your Spirit. Amen.

MEDITATION SEVENTEEN
PRAYING WITH GROANS AND SIGHS

IF the soul is to pray rightly, it must pray with the help and strength of the Holy Spirit, because it is impossible for a person to express himself in prayer without the Spirit. When I say it is impossible for a person to express himself in prayer without the Spirit, I mean that it is impossible for the heart, in a sincere and sensible way, to pour itself out before God with those groans and sighs that come from a truly praying heart.

The mouth is not the main thing to be looked to in prayer. What counts is whether the heart is so full of passion and earnestness in prayer that it is impossible to express its feeling and desire in words. When a person desires deeply, when his desires are so strong and mighty that all the tears, groans, and words that can come from the heart cannot be uttered, then "the Spirit helps us in our weakness. We do not know what we ought to pray for, but the Spirit himself intercedes for us with groans that words cannot express" (Rom. 8:26).

A poor prayer is just so many words. A person who *truly prays* one prayer shall after that never be able to express with his mouth or pen the unutterable desires, feelings, and longing that went to God in that prayer.

The best prayers have often more groans than words. And those words that it has are but a lean and shallow representation of the heart, life, and spirit of that prayer. You do not find any words of prayer, that we read of, come out of the mouth of Moses, when he was going out of Egypt, and was followed by Pharaoh, and yet he made heaven ring again with his cry: "Then the Lord said to Moses, 'Why are you crying out to me? Tell the Israelites to move on' " (Exod. 14:15). Moses released inexpressible and unsearchable groans and cryings of his soul in and with the Spirit. God is the God of spirits, and his eyes look further than at the outside of any duty whatsoever: "But Moses and Aaron fell facedown and cried out, 'O God, God of the spirits of all mankind, will you be angry with the entire assembly when only one man sins?' " (Num. 16:22). I doubt that this is thought of by most of those who would be looked upon as a praying people.

The nearer a person comes to fulfilling any work that God has commanded him to do according to his will, so much the more hard and difficult it is. And the reason is that man by himself is not able to do it; he must have the aid of the Holy Spirit. Now prayer is not only a duty, but one of the most eminent of duties; and therefore, so much the more difficult. Paul understood this, for he said, "I will pray with the Spirit." He knew well that it was not what others wrote or said that could make him a praying person. Nothing less than the Spirit could do it.

PRAYER

O Lord, I do groan and sigh when I think of the immense tasks and responsibilities you have laid upon my shoulders. I groan and sigh because I know too well my failings and inadequacies. I groan and sigh, but I take hope in the promise that in my groans and confessions I am strengthened and forgiven and I am empowered and prayed for by your Spirit. I groan and I sigh, but I know full well that your yoke is easy and your burden is light compared to my trying to live and work without you. I praise you that I have experienced the difference between slavery in fear and service in friendship with you. May I never forget my need of your Spirit each moment of my life, and when I am groaning and sighing may I be encouraged with the knowledge that you are there praying with me and for me through Jesus Christ my Savior. Amen.

MEDITATION EIGHTEEN
PRAY WITHOUT FAINTING

TRUE prayer must be with the Holy Spirit, or else there will be a failing in the very act of prayer itself, a fainting in the execution of the work. Prayer is an ordinance of God that must continue with a person as long as he is on this side of glory. But as I said before, it is not possible for a person to lift up his heart to God in prayer, nor keep it there, without the assistance of the Spirit. And for a person to continue from time to time in prayer with God, he must be with the Spirit.

Christ tells us that people ought always to pray and not grow weary: "Then Jesus told his disciples a parable to show them that they should always pray and not give up" (Luke 18:1). The Scriptures tell us that a hypocrite is a person who either will not continue in prayer, or, if he does, his prayer will not be in the power, that is, in the spirit of prayer, but for a pretense only: "Will he find delight in the Almighty? Will he call upon God at all times?" (Job 27:10). For this fault, among others, Jesus declared that hypocrites would suffer many woes (Matt. 23). It is the easiest thing for a hundred people to turn prayer into a mere ritual or formality, but it is the hardest thing for one person to keep himself fixed on any one duty, especially prayer. Prayer is such a duty and work that a person without the help of the Spirit cannot so much as pray once, much less continue, without him. The Holy Spirit inspires in us a sweet praying frame of mind; and in praying, he helps us so to pray as to have our prayers ascend into the ears of the Lord God.

Jacob did not only begin his prayer, but he held to it: "I will not let you go unless you bless me" (Gen. 32:26). This is so of the godly: "He struggled with the angel and overcame him; he wept and begged for his favor. He found him at Bethel and talked with him there—the LORD God Almighty, the LORD is his name of renown! But you must return to your God; maintain love and justice, and wait for your God always" (Hos. 12:4-6). But this could not be without the Spirit in prayer: "For through him we both have access to the Father by one Spirit" (Eph. 2:18).

The same thing is found in the Epistle of Jude, where the saints are urged to pray, to stand fast, and to continue to hold out in the faith of the gospel. Prayer was an excellent means for holding on to faith, without which he knew they would never be able to do it. Jude wrote: "But you, dear friends, build yourselves up in your most holy faith and pray in the Holy Spirit" (Jude 20). It is as if he had said, "Brethren, as eternal life is laid up only for the people who hold out, so you cannot hold out unless you continue praying in the Holy Spirit." The great cheat that the Devil and the antichrist delude the world with is to keep people in the formality of any duty apart from the Spirit—that is, to make praying and preaching into mere mechanical rituals. There are many people who have a form of godliness, but deny its power and turn away (see 2 Tim. 3:5). They make worship into a hollow ritual. But true prayer must be much more than ritual.

PRAYER

O Holy Father, send your Holy Spirit and fill me again with the power of prayer and service. Empower me to endure when exhaustion or even the cares of this world would pull me away from my time of communion with you. May I be certain that salvation rests only in you, and that I can bring the gospel to others in word and deed only if you be with me strengthening me so that the work is really your work and not mine. May I be certain of these things in my mind, that I might truly stay with you in faith with my whole heart and soul, through Jesus Christ our Lord. Amen.

MEDITATION NINETEEN
PRAY IN SPIRIT AND MIND

WHAT is it to pray with the spirit and to pray with the understanding also? The Apostle Paul puts a clear distinction between praying with the spirit, and praying with the spirit *and* with the understanding. Therefore he wrote that he would "pray with my spirit," but then he added, "but I will also pray with my mind." This distinction was occasioned through the Corinthians not observing that it was their duty to do what they did to the edification of themselves and others too: they were praying for their own commendation. Many of them had extraordinary gifts —such as speaking in different tongues—but they were more concerned about possessing these gifts than they were about the edifying of their brethren. This made Paul write to them to let them understand that though extraordinary gifts were excellent, yet to act for the edification of the church was more excellent. Said the Apostle, "For if I pray in a tongue, my spirit prays, but my mind is unfruitful. So what shall I do? I will pray with my spirit, but I will also pray with my mind; I will sing with my spirit, but I will also sing with my mind. . . . But in the church I would rather speak five intelligible words to instruct others than ten thousand words in a tongue" (1 Cor. 14:14, 15, 19).

It is expedient then that the understanding—the mind—should be occupied in prayer, as well as the heart and mouth. That which is done with understanding is done more effectively, sensibly, and heartily than that which is done without it. This truth made the Apostle pray for the Colossians that God would fill them with "the knowledge of his will through all spiritual wisdom and understanding" (Col. 1:9). And for the Ephesians he prayed that God would give to them "the Spirit of wisdom and revelation, so that you may know him better" (Eph. 1:17). He prayed for the Philippians that God would make them abound "more and more in knowledge and depth of insight, so that you may be able to discern what is best and may be pure and blameless until the day of Christ, filled with the fruit of righteousness that comes through Jesus Christ—to the glory and praise of God" (Phil. 1:9-11).

Properly exercised, the mind is helpful in everything a person undertakes, either civil or spiritual; therefore, a clear understanding must be desired by all who would be praying people. In the following pages, I will show you what it is to pray with the mind, and I will do this experimentally. For the making of right prayers, it is required that there should be a spiritual understanding in all those who pray to God.

To pray with the understanding—the mind—is to pray while being instructed by the Spirit regarding those things you are to pray for. Though you are in much need of pardon for sin and deliverance from the wrath to come, if you do not understand this, you will either not desire these things or else you will be so lukewarm in your desires after them that God will loathe your asking for them. Thus it was with the church of Laodicea. They lacked knowledge or spiritual understanding; they did not know that they were so poor, wretched, blind, and naked. Their lack of spiritual understanding made them and all their services so loathsome to Christ that he threatened to spew them out of his mouth (Rev. 3:16, 17).

Men without understanding may say the same words in prayer as others do, but if there is understanding in one man and none in the other, there is a mighty difference in speaking the very same words! The one speaking from a spiritual understanding will know far more in the receiving or in the denying of his desires than the other who prays in words only without the understanding.

Spiritual understanding should see in the heart of God a readiness and a willingness to give those things to the soul that the soul stands in need of. David by spiritual understanding could comprehend the very thoughts of God toward him. And thus it was with the Canaanite woman: she did by faith and a right understanding discern, beyond the seemingly harsh words of Christ to her, tenderness and willingness in his heart to save her daughter. This understanding caused her to be earnest and restless until she could enjoy the mercy she stood in need of (Matt. 15:22-28).

Spiritual understanding, understanding the willingness that is in the heart of God to save sinners, will press the soul to seek after God and to cry for pardon. If a man should see a pearl worth a thousand dollars lying in a ditch and not understand the value of it, he would lightly pass it by. But if he once got knowledge of its value, he would venture in up to the neck to get it. So it is with souls concerning the things of God. If a man once gets an understanding of the worth of them, then his heart runs after them. And he will never stop crying for them until he has them. The two blind men in the gospel, because they did certainly know that Jesus, who was going by them, was both able and willing to heal such infirmities as they were afflicted with, cried out. And the more they were rebuked, the more they cried out until he heard and answered their needs (Matt. 20:29-31).

PRAYER

O Father, too often I lack spiritual discernment and I am not even aware of it! I do not understand the needs of my soul. Too often, I blunder on in prayer, requesting things I do not need or things that would hurt me or others. Help me to pray from an understanding heart that does not just mouth words. Help me to perceive your answers to prayer when they are given or when my requests are denied for good reasons. Inspire me to praise you for all things, and thank you for both your gifts and your denials of my requests. Enlighten my mind by the special influence of your Spirit to see the signs of the times and then pray for exactly what you are seeking to do for me and for others in answer to heartfelt prayers. I pray these things in the name of Jesus, who came to bring truth into the world and be the way to you. Amen.

MEDITATION TWENTY
REASON WITH GOD

A PERSON with enlightened understanding will see many and varied applications of the promises of God from Scripture to encourage him to pray. The understanding adds to God's promises so that a person can pray from "strength to strength." The psalmist knew this from personal experience: "As they pass through the Valley of Baca [Valley of Sorrow], they make it a place of springs; the autumn rains also cover it with pools. They go from strength to strength till each appears before God in Zion" (Ps. 84:6, 7). The psalmist knew that in times and places of difficulty God would hear his prayers and give him strength to overcome his troubles. He could claim God's promises in prayer to find a way of deliverance, knowing that God is faithful in keeping his word. It is a great encouragement to know what promises God has made to his people, so that his people can come and ask for them.

When your mind is enlightened, you can come to God with suitable arguments or reasons regarding why he should answer your requests. Jacob reasoned with God in prayer on the basis of his promise to him: "Then Jacob prayed, 'O God of my father Abraham, God of my father

Isaac, O LORD, who said to me, "Go back to your country and your relatives, and I will make you prosper," I am unworthy of all the kindness and faithfulness you have shown your servant. I had only my staff when I crossed this Jordan, but now I have become two groups. Save me, I pray, from the hand of my brother Esau, for I am afraid he will come and attack me, and also the mothers with their children. But you have said, "I will surely make you prosper and will make your descendants like the sand of the sea, which cannot be counted" ' " (Gen. 32:9-12). Sometimes in a prayer of supplication—not in a verbal prayer only, but even a silent prayer from the heart—the Holy Spirit will force through the understanding such effective arguments that you will move the heart of God.

When Ephraim—that is, Israel—got a right understanding of its unseemly conduct toward the Lord, it began to grieve. In grieving over its sins, Ephraim used such arguments with the Lord that it affected his heart, drew out his forgiveness, and made Ephraim pleasant in his eyes. God declared through his prophet Jeremiah, " 'I have surely heard Ephraim's moaning: "You disciplined me like an unruly calf, and I have been disciplined. Restore me, and I will return, because you are the LORD my God. After I strayed, I repented; after I came to understand, I beat my breast. I was ashamed and humiliated because I bore the disgrace of my youth." Is not Ephraim my dear son, the child in whom I delight? Though I often speak against him, I still remember him. Therefore my heart yearns for him; I have great compassion for him,' declares the Lord" (Jer. 31:18-20). Thus you see that just as it is required to pray with the Spirit, so it is required to pray with the understanding also.

To illustrate what has just been said, suppose that two beggars come to your door. One of them is a poor, lame, wounded, and starved creature; and the other is a healthy and vigorous person. These two use the same words in their begging: the one says that he is almost starved and so does the other. But the one who is indeed poor, lame, wounded, and almost starved speaks with more feeling and more of an understanding of what is mentioned in their begging than does the other one. You are able to discern the lame one by his more emotional speaking and his bemoaning himself. His pain and poverty make him speak more in a spirit of lamentation than the other, and he shall be pitied sooner than the other by all those who have the least dram of natural compassion or pity. Thus it is with God: there are some who out of custom and formality go and pray; there are others who go in the bitterness of their spirits. The one prays out of mere habit, as a ritual. The other has his words forced from him by the anguish of his soul. Surely the latter is the man that God will look at and listen to—the one who is poor, the one who has a humble and contrite spirit before the Lord, the one who hears and understands his Word and trembles: " 'This is the one I esteem: he who is humble and contrite in spirit, and trembles at my word' " (Isa. 66:2).

PRAYER

Dear heavenly Father, help me to understand myself when I come to you in prayer. Help me to understand your Word and the promises you have made to all Christians. Search me, O Lord, and show me my heart and deepest longings, reveal to me the exact nature of my wrongs. May your Holy Spirit empower me to truly open myself before you with honesty that I might confess my sins and find forgiveness through faith in Jesus Christ and his redeeming work. You have promised, O God, that if I will confess my sins, then you will be faithful and just and forgive me of all my sins. I claim that promise for my life, and I pray that your Holy Spirit would apply the assurance of your forgiveness to my heart and understanding, for Jesus' sake. Amen.

MEDITATION TWENTY-ONE
THE ENLIGHTENED MIND

A WELL-ENLIGHTENED understanding is of admirable use in regard to the manner and matter of prayer. He that has his understanding well exercised to discern between good and evil, and a sense either of the misery of man or the mercy of God, does not need the writings of other men to teach him prayer by forms. A person who feels pain does not need to be taught to cry, "Oh!" Likewise, a person who has his understanding opened by the Spirit does not need to be taught by other men's prayers, so that he can only slavishly repeat what others have already said. The present sense, feeling, and pressure that lie upon his spirit provoke him to groan out his own heartfelt request to the Lord.

When the psalmist had the pains of hell catching hold of him, and the sorrows of hell compassing about him, he did not need any church official or any other person to teach him to say, "O Lord, save me!" He said, "The cords of death entangled me, the anguish of the grave came upon me; I was overcome by trouble and sorrow. Then I called on the name of the LORD: 'O LORD, save me!' The LORD is gracious and righteous; our God is full of compassion. The LORD protects the simplehearted; when I was in great need, he saved me" (Ps. 116:3-6). The psalmist didn't look into a book of rituals to teach him a certain form to use to pour out his heart before God. It is the nature of the heart of sick men, in their pain and sickness, to give expression to sorrowful groans and complainings to those who stand by them. This was true of David in Psalm 38: "O LORD, do not forsake me; be not far from me, O my God. Come quickly to help me, O Lord my Savior" (Ps. 38:21, 22). And thus, blessed be the Lord, it is the same with all those who are endowed with the grace of God.

It is necessary that there be an enlightened understanding, to the end that the soul be kept in the continuation of the duty of prayer.

The people of God are not ignorant of how many wiles, tricks, and temptations the devil has to make upon a poor soul, who is truly willing to have the Lord Jesus Christ as his Savior. The Devil tempts that soul to be weary of seeking the face of God, and to think that God is not willing to show mercy. "Yes," says Satan, "you may pray indeed, but you shall not prevail. You see your heart is hard, cold, dull, and dead. You do not pray with the Spirit. You do not pray earnestly. Your thoughts are running after other things, when you pretend to pray to God. Away, hypocrite! Go no further! It is in vain to strive any longer!" After this, if you are not well-informed in your understanding, you will presently cry out, "The LORD has forsaken me, the Lord has forgotten me" (Isa. 49:14). But if you are rightly informed and enlightened, you will say, "I will seek the Lord, and wait; I will not stop praying though the Lord keeps silent for a time and speaks not a word of comfort." He loved Jacob dearly, and yet he made him wrestle before he had the blessing (Gen. 32; Isa. 40). Seeming delays in

God are not tokens of his displeasure. He may hide his face from his dearest saints. "I will wait for the LORD, who is hiding his face from the house of Jacob. I will put my trust in him" (Isa. 8:17). He loves to help keep his people in prayer. He loves to find them ever knocking at the gate of heaven. "It may be," you can reason, "the Lord is testing me, or he loves to hear me speak of my sad condition before him and solely rest upon him for my needs."

PRAYER

Dear heavenly Father, I thank you that you desire honesty of expression in my prayer life. I thank you that I do not have to put on a hypocritical smiling front when I am in the deepest agony, but I can come to you just as I am in Jesus Christ. O Lord, I thank you because I am so aware of my personal shortcomings, inadequacies, and sins that sometimes I can only groan when I pray. Indeed, I am aware that you look upon my groanings, honest moans from my soul, as real honest prayers. Thank you, God, for hearing my groans as prayers. Now send your Holy Spirit in your redeeming love to remove the agony of my spirit and mind. I cannot form words to express my real spiritual needs, but you can see into my heart—so answer me! Through Jesus Christ, your Son, who knew the agonies of prayer. Amen.

MEDITATION TWENTY-TWO
PATIENCE IN PRAYER

THE Canaanite woman who asked Jesus to heal her daughter would not take *seeming denials* for real ones (Matt. 15:22-28). She knew that the Lord was gracious, and that though he declared that his mission was to the Jews and not the Gentiles, he would show compassion to any who earnestly pleaded.

In Luke's Gospel we read again of the importance of pleading with the Lord and waiting for his mercy.

> Then Jesus told his disciples a parable to show them that they should always pray and not give up. He said: "In a certain town there was a judge who neither feared God nor cared about men. And there was a widow in that town who kept coming to him with the plea, 'Grant me justice against my adversary.' For some time he refused. But finally he said to himself, 'Even though I don't fear God or care about men, yet because this widow keeps bothering me, I will see that she gets justice, so that she won't eventually wear me out with her coming!' " And the Lord said, "Listen to what the unjust judge says. And will not God bring about justice for his chosen ones, who cry out to him day and night? Will he keep putting them off?" (Luke 18:1-7).

We do well to wait upon the Lord's mercy. After all, the Lord has waited a lot longer upon us than we have waited upon him! "I waited patiently for the LORD;" David said, "he turned to me and heard my cry" (Ps. 40:1). And the best help in patient waiting is an understanding well-informed and enlightened.

Alas! How many poor souls are there in the world, who, because they are not well-informed in their understanding, are often ready to give up all for lost because of the tricks and temptations of Satan! The Lord pity them! The Lord help them to pray with the spirit and with the understanding also. This is true to much of my own experiences. When I have been in my fits of agony of spirit, I have often been strongly persuaded to quit and to ask the Lord no longer to answer my request. But then I remember and understand what great sinners the Lord has had mercy upon, and how large his promises are still to sinners. And I remember that it was not the whole and healthy, but the sick; not the righteous, but the sinners; not the full, but the empty that he intended to give his grace and mercy. When I remember these things, my patience is renewed and I persevere in prayer until I receive the blessing. Remembering and understanding the teachings of the Scriptures has made me—through the assistance of the Holy Spirit—cleave to him, hang upon him, and continue to cry, though for the present he made no answer—and he has helped me! May the Lord help all of his poor, tempted, and afflicted people to do the same and to continue, though it be long, according to the saying of the prophet: "For the revelation awaits an appointed time; it speaks of the end and will not prove false. Though it linger, wait for it; it will certainly come and not delay" (Hab. 2:3). May the Lord help those to pray to that end, not by the inventions of men and their rituals, but with the spirit and the understanding also.

PRAYER

O Lord, teach me patience and endurance in my prayers. Teach me not only those things I am to pray for, but teach me the promises of Scripture which I may claim as I pray. Guide me with your Spirit in my heartfelt pleas for answers to my prayers. Grant me understanding when I pray day after day and you postpone your answer. O Lord, I thank you for your goodness and mercy. Help me to glorify and honor you before men and angels, even when my requests are not immediately fulfilled. Help me in all things and in all circumstances to live and pray as a Christian so others may see and understand you and your Good News for all. Amen.

MEDITATION TWENTY-THREE
WHEN YOU TRY BUT CANNOT PRAY

NOW some of you may have experienced going into secret and intending to pray and to pour out your soul before God, but found that you could scarcely pray anything at all.

Ah! Sweet soul! It is not your words that are important to God. He will not mind if you cannot come to him with some eloquent oration. His eye is on the brokenness of your heart; this is what makes the very heart of God run over. "The sacrifices of God are a broken spirit; a broken and contrite heart, O God, you will not despise" (Ps. 51:17).

The stopping of your words to God may arise from too much trouble in your heart. David was so troubled sometimes that he could not speak: "I remembered you, O God, and I groaned; I mused, and my spirit grew faint. You kept my eyes from closing; I was too troubled to speak" (Ps. 77:3, 4). But this might comfort all sorrowful hearts, that though you cannot through the anguish of your spirit speak much, yet the Holy Spirit stirs up in your heart groans and sighs so much more effectively. When your mouth is hindered, yet your spirit is not hindered. Moses made heaven ring with his prayers in his deepest agony

104

of heart, yet not one word came from his mouth.

If you would more fully express yourself before the Lord, study: first, study your sinful condition; second, study God's promises; and third, study the loving heart of Christ. You may discern the heart of Christ by pondering his condescension and shed blood. You may think of the mercy he has shown to sinners in former times. Then in your prayer plead your own sinfulness and unworthiness, bemoan your condition before God, plead Christ's shed blood, plead for the mercy that he extended to other sinners, plead with his many rich promises of grace, and let these things be upon your heart in your meditations.

Yet, let me still counsel you. Take heed that you do not content yourself with mere words. Take heed lest you think that God looks only upon your words. Whether your words be few or many, let your heart and soul go with them to God. You shall seek and find him when you seek him with your whole heart and being: " 'For I know the plans I have for you,' declares the LORD, 'plans to prosper you and not to harm you, plans to give you hope and a future. Then you will call upon me and come and pray to me, and I will listen to you. You will seek me and find me when you seek me with all your heart' " (Jer. 29:11-13).

PRAYER

O Lord, I have not known how to come to you when I have been feeling the condemnation of my sin. I have not felt able to ask you for blessing when I have harbored unconfessed sin. By the Holy Spirit's help, aid me to examine my life and the depths of my heart so I can confess my sins and be forgiven. Create in me a clean heart so I can work and pray from pure motives and intentions. Lift me up so I might see how precious Christ is, experience his redeeming love in my heart, and be empowered to serve him with greater boldness. Amen.

MEDITATION TWENTY-FOUR
PRAY FOR THE HOLY SPIRIT

CHRIST bids us to pray for the Spirit, but this implies that a person without the Spirit may pray and be heard:

> "So I say to you: Ask and it will be given to you; seek and you will find; knock and the door will be opened to you. For everyone who asks receives; he who seeks finds; and to him who knocks, the door will be opened. Which of you fathers, if your son asks for a fish, will give him a snake instead? Or if he asks for an egg, will give him a scorpion? If you then, though you are evil, know how to give good gifts to your children, how much more will your Father in heaven give the Holy Spirit to those who ask him!" (Luke 11:9-13).

The speech of Christ in this passage is directed to his own disciples. Christ is telling them that God would give his Holy Spirit to those who ask him and he is to be understood as meaning to get *more* of the Holy Spirit. Since they are the disciples who are spoken to, they had a measure of the Spirit already. He had told his disciples to pray "Our Father." Christians ought to pray for the Holy Spirit; that is, they should pray for *more* of him, though

God has endowed them with the Spirit already.

I might be asked, "Would you have no one pray except those who know that they are disciples of Christ?" I answer, "Let every soul that would be saved pour out his soul to God."

I know that if the grace of God is in you, it will be natural for you to groan out your condition to God, as natural as it is for a nursing child to cry out for the breast of his mother. Genuine prayer is one of the first things to reveal that a man is a Christian. But yet, if it be the right kind of prayer it will be as follows:

1. Right prayer must desire God in Christ, for himself; for his holiness, love, wisdom, and glory. Right prayer will run to God only through Christ, so that it will center on God and on God alone. As the psalmist has prayed: "Whom have I in heaven but you? And being with you, I desire nothing on earth" (Ps. 73:25).

2. Right prayer must enjoy continually communion with him, both here and hereafter. "And I—in righteousness I will see your face; when I awake, I will be satisfied with seeing your likeness" (Ps. 17:15). And as Paul wrote, "Meanwhile we groan" (2 Cor. 5:2).

3. Right prayer is accompanied with a continual labor after that which is prayed for. "My soul waits for the Lord more than watchmen wait for the morning" (Ps. 130:6). For note, I beseech you, *there are two things that provoke to prayer. The one is a detestation of sin and the things of this life; the other is a burning desire for communion with God, in a holy and undefiled state and inheritance.* Compare but this one thing with most of the prayers that are made by men, and you shall find them but mock prayers, and the breathings of an abominable spirit. For most men either do not pray at all, or else only endeavor to mock God and the world by doing so. Compare their prayer and the course

of their lives together, and you may easily see that the thing included in their prayer is the thing least looked after in their lives. To pray rightly we must pray knowing every good thing comes from God. But we must also work hard so the Spirit of God can very often achieve his purpose through us. God wants our prayer life to be consistent and our outward visible life to be a demonstration of our inner spiritual life.

PRAYER

O Lord, I thank you for the gift of your Holy Spirit in my life, but I confess that I have often pushed him off into a corner of my life and I have grieved him for my disregard of him. Forgive me for my selfishness and my insensitivity to the spiritual blessings you would have me enjoy, because I have been too much concerned with worldly matters. Fill me now with the fullness of your Spirit, not for my selfish enjoyment, but for my communion with you—that will lead to your praise and glory. Fill me with your Spirit now, that I might live a life consistent with my profession of faith in Jesus Christ. Amen.

MEDITATION TWENTY-FIVE
PRAYER IN FEAR AND HOPE

AS prayer is the duty of every one of the children of God, and since it is to be carried on by the Spirit of Christ in the soul, so everyone who offers to take upon himself to pray to the Lord needs to be wary and go about the work especially with the fear of God, as well as with the hope of the mercy of God through Christ.

Prayer is an ordinance of God in which a man draws very near to God. Therefore, prayer calls so much more for the assistance of the grace of God to help a soul to pray, because in prayer you are especially in the presence of God.

It is a shame for a man to behave himself irreverently before a king, but it is a sin to behave so before God! And as a king, if wise, is not pleased with an oration made up of unseemly or empty words and gestures, so God takes no pleasure in the sacrifice of fools:

> Guard your steps when you go to the house of God. Go near to listen rather than to offer the sacrifice of fools, who do not know that they are wrong. Do not be quick with your mouth, do not be hasty in your heart to utter anything before God. God is in heaven and you are on

earth, so let your words be few. As a dream comes when there are many cares, so the speech of a fool when there are many words. When you make a vow to God, do not delay in fulfilling it. He has no pleasure in fools; fulfill your vow (Eccles. 5:1-4).

Neither long discourses nor eloquent tongues are pleasing to the ear of God, but a humble, broken and contrite heart is sweet in the sight of the heavenly Majesty: "For this is what the high and lofty One says—he who lives forever, whose name is holy: 'I live in a high and holy place, but also with him who is contrite and lowly in spirit, to revive the spirit of the lowly and to revive the heart of the contrite' " (Isa. 57:15). In some of the following pages I will discuss the chief obstructions to right prayer.

When men bear iniquity in their hearts, at the time of their prayers before God, it is as though a great impenetrable wall is separating them from God. "If I had cherished sin in my heart," said the psalmist, "the Lord would not have listened; but God has surely listened and heard my voice in prayer" (Ps. 66:18, 19).

You must understand this: you may pray for the preventing of temptation while at the same time you have a secret love for the very thing which you are praying to resist and are asking strength against. This shows the wickedness of man's heart, which will even love and hold fast to that which with the mouth it prays against. Of this sort are those who honor God with their mouths, but their hearts are far from him: "My people come to you, as they usually do, and sit before you to listen to your words, but they do not put them into practice. With their mouths they express devotion, but their hearts are greedy for unjust gain" (Ezek. 33:31).

How ugly it would be in our eyes if we should see a

beggar ask for alms with the intention of throwing it to the dogs! Or think of that man who prays with one breath, "Bestow this upon me," and with the next breath, "I beseech you, do not give it to me!" And thus it is with those people who say with their mouths, "Your will be done," and with their hearts they mean everything else. With their mouths they say, "Hallowed be your name," and with their hearts and lives they delight to dishonor him all the day long. These are the *prayers that become sin*, and though they are prayed often, the Lord will never answer them. "They cried for help, but there was no one to save them—to the LORD, but he did not answer" (2 Sam. 22:42).

When men pray for show to be heard, and to be thought a somebody in religion, and the like, these prayers also fall short of God's approbation and are never likely to be answered in reference to eternal life. There are those who seek repute and applause for their eloquent words and who seek more to tickle the ears and heads of their hearers more than anything else. These people pray to be heard by men, and have all of their reward already (Matt. 6:5). You can discover these persons by these marks:

1. Their concern is only for their auditory expressions.

2. They look for commendation when they are done.

3. Their hearts either rise or fall according to their praise or amount of enlargement.

4. The length of their prayers pleases them, and in order for their prayers to be long they will vainly repeat things over and over again (Matt. 6:7).

5. When their prayers are over, they wait not to hear from God but from man.

God loves to hear our prayers and answer our every request. God wants to be personally involved in our lives, and will be involved when we love him and honor him for what he is.

PRAYER

Father, search me and know me. Reveal to me the hidden secrets of my heart. Show me the sin which I still love, and convict me by your Spirit of all unrighteousness. Aid me to turn from all unrighteousness to you with the resolve to be obedient in all things. Forgive me and enable me to live moment by moment in love and faith. May these words of mine not be so much for the hearts and minds of others, but may they be from my heart to you and help others to give their hearts to you as well. Amen.

MEDITATION TWENTY-SIX
PRAYER THAT ASSURES NO ANSWER

MEDITATION TWENTY-SIX

PRAYER THAT

PRAYER that God will not accept and answer is prayer which is for the wrong things—or, if for the right things, the prayer is with the wrong motives. Some people come to God in prayer for that which they can spend upon their selfish wants or for the wrong ends. Some have not because they ask not, and others ask and have not because they ask amiss, wanting only what will satisfy their selfish desires:

> You want something but don't get it. You kill and covet, but you cannot have what you want. You quarrel and fight. You do not have, because you do not ask God. When you ask, you do not receive, because you ask with wrong motives, that you may spend what you get on your pleasures. You adulterous people, don't you know that friendship with the world is hatred toward God? Anyone who chooses to be a friend of the world becomes an enemy of God (James 4:2-4).

Goals contrary to God's will are a great argument with God for him to not answer your petitions. Hence it is that so many pray for this or that, and yet receive not. God answers them only with silence; they have their words for their labor—and that is all. Now some might object and say that God does hear some persons, though their hearts be not right with him, as he did Israel. He gave them quails in the wilderness, though they spent them upon their lusts. If God does this, it is in judgment and not in mercy. He gave them their desire indeed, but they would have been better without it, for he also sent leanness into their souls. Woe be to that man when God answers him in such a way! As the psalmist explains: "Then they believed his promises and sang his praise. But they soon forgot what he had done and did not wait for his counsel. In the desert they gave in to their craving; in the wasteland they put God to the test. So he gave them what they asked for, but sent a wasting disease upon them" (Ps. 106:12-15).

There are other sorts of prayers that are not answered. These are the prayers that are made by men and presented to God in their own persons only, without their appearing in the Lord Jesus. For though God has appointed prayer, and promised to hear the prayers of his creatures, yet he will not hear the prayer of any creature if he does not come in Christ. Jesus has told us, "And I will do whatever you ask in my name, so that the Son may bring glory to the Father" (John 14:13). And as Paul has written, "And whatever you do, whether in word or deed, do it all in the name of the Lord Jesus, giving thanks to God the Father through him" (Col. 3:17). Though you might be devout, earnest, zealous, and constant in prayer, yet it is in Christ only that you will be heard and accepted.

But alas! Most people do not know what it is to come to God in the name of the Lord Jesus. And that is the reason why they live wicked, pray wicked, and die wicked.

Come now to your Father in heaven. Come in the name of his Son and receive his mercy and lovingkindness. God is more than willing to give us all that we can ask when we have dedicated all that we have to his service.

PRAYER

O Lord, help me to pray with right motives and intentions in my heart. Help me to never ask for things so that I can simply spend those things upon my selfish desires or for the increase of my pleasures. Instead of praying wrongly, help me to know you so well that I will pray only for those things that you would want me to have and pray for. Help me to pray for those things that are according to your will and intentions each day. Father, you see the larger scene. You see and understand my real needs and the needs of others. You know the real needs of your kingdom on earth. Help me to pray for and be your co-worker in all of these things that you see so clearly. Fill me with your Holy Spirit so that I can pray in Jesus' name and make a real difference in the world. I offer this prayer not in my own righteousness, but in the righteousness of your Son who died for me. Amen.

MEDITATION TWENTY-SEVEN
PRAYER MUST HAVE POWER

THE last thing which hinders prayer is the *form* of prayer without the *power*. It is an easy thing for men to be very hot for such things as rituals and forms of prayer as they are written in a book. Yet they are altogether forgetful to inquire within themselves whether or not they have the spirit and power of prayer. These people are like painted men, and their prayers are like a false voice. They appear as hypocrites to God, and their prayers are an abomination: "If any man turns a deaf ear to the law, even his prayers are detestable" (Prov. 28:9). When they say they have been pouring out their souls to God, he says that they have been howling like dogs: "They do not cry out to me from their hearts but wail upon their beds. They gather together for grain and new wine but turn away from me" (Hos. 7:14).

When therefore you intend to pray to the Lord of heaven and earth, consider the following particulars:

1. Consider seriously what you want. Do not, as many who in their words only beat the air, ask for such things as indeed you do not desire, nor see that you stand in need of.

2. When you see what you want, keep to that and take heed to pray sensibly.

3. Take heed that your heart as well as your mouth speaks to God. Let not your mouth go any further than you strive to draw out your heart along with it. David would lift his heart and soul to the Lord; and for good reason, for so far as a man's mouth goes along without his heart, so far his prayer is but lip-labor only. If you have in mind to enlarge in prayer before God, see to it that it be with your heart.

4. Avoid just affecting expressions and pleasing yourself with their use, because you can quickly forget the real life of prayer.

Real prayer is a serious concern, for we are speaking to the Sovereign Lord of all the universe, who is willing to move heaven and earth in answer to sincere and reasonable prayer. Prayer is not a mechanical duty, but a wonderful opportunity to develop a loving and caring relationship with the most important Person in our lives.

PRAYER

Father, my prayer to you will never have power without the Holy Spirit filling my life and until I really begin to praise you for who you are and for what you are doing according to your holy character. I love you for creating the wonder of life and the beauty of creation. I thank you for the Word that proclaims many things which are hidden from those who think they are wise in their own eyes, but which makes wise those who are humble and contrite of heart. Grant me power in prayer by giving me a greater awareness of your wonder, majesty, and love in Christ Jesus. Amen.

MEDITATION TWENTY-EIGHT
A WORD OF ENCOURAGEMENT

TAKE heed that you do not throw off prayer through sudden persuasions that you do not have the Holy Spirit. It is the great work of the Devil to do his best, or rather worst, against the best prayers. He will flatter false dissembling hypocrites and feed them with a thousand fancies of well-doing, when their very duties of prayer, and all their other duties as well, stink in the nostrils of God. The Devil will also stand at a man's side to persuade him that neither his person nor his performance are accepted by God. Such an instance occurs in the Book of Zechariah:

> Then he showed me Joshua the high priest standing before the angel of the LORD, and Satan standing at his right side to accuse him. The LORD said to Satan, "The LORD rebuke you, Satan! The LORD, who has chosen Jerusalem, rebuke you! Is not this man a burning stick snatched from the fire?" Now Joshua was dressed in filthy clothes as he stood before the angel. The angel said to those who were standing before him, "Take off his filthy clothes." Then he said to Joshua, "See, I have taken away your sin, and I will put rich garments on you." Then I said, "Put a clean turban on his head." So they put a clean turban on his head and clothed him,

while the angel of the LORD stood by. The angel of the LORD gave this charge to Joshua: "This is what the LORD Almighty says: 'If you will walk in my ways and keep my requirements, then you will govern my house and have charge of my courts, and I will give you a place among those standing here' " (Zech. 3:1-7).

Take heed, therefore, of such false conclusions and groundless discouragements brought on by Satan. If such persuasions do come in upon your spirit to convince you that you cannot pray, rather than being discouraged by them, use them to put yourself into greater sincerity and restlessness of spirit when you approach God.

As such sudden temptations should not stop you from prayer and pouring out your soul to God, so neither should your own heart's corruptions hinder you. It may be that you find within all those corruptions before mentioned, and they may be endeavoring to put themselves in you when you seek to pray to him. Your business then is to judge them and to pray against them. Lay yourself much more at the foot of God in a sense of your own sinfulness rather than arguing for your requests from the corruption of your heart. Plead with God for justifying and sanctifying grace, and don't argue from discouragement and despair. David prayed this way: "For the sake of your name, O LORD, forgive my iniquity, though it be great" (Ps. 25:11).

I would like to speak a word of encouragement to the poor, tempted, and cast down soul to pray to God in Christ. Though all prayer that is accepted by God in reference to eternal life must be in the Spirit—for that alone makes intercession for us according to the will of God—yet because many poor souls may have the Holy Spirit working on them, and stirring them up to groan unto the Lord for mercy, they may pray to God through Christ. Even though through unbelief they do not, nor for the present cannot, believe that they are the people of God, such people as he delights in, still the truth of grace may be coming upon them.

That Scripture in Luke 11 is very encouraging to any poor soul who hungers after Jesus Christ. In verse 5-7, Jesus speaks a parable about a man who went to his friend to borrow three loaves. The friend, because he was in bed, denied him the loaves; yet for the man's persistence, the friend rose and gave him what he asked. This parable clearly signifies that though poor souls, through the weakness of their faith, cannot see that they are the friends of God, yet they should never quit asking, seeking, and knocking at God's door for mercy. Poor heart! You cry out that God will not regard you, for you believe that you are not a friend to him but rather an enemy in your heart through wicked words and works. And you are as though you heard the Lord saying to you: "Trouble me not! I cannot give to you as to the one in the parable." Yet you should continue knocking, crying, moaning, and wailing. My own experience tells me that nothing will so prevail with God as pleading. Is it not so with you respecting beggars who come to your door? Though you have no heart to give them anything at their first asking, yet if they follow you bemoaning themselves, won't you give to them? Scripture tells us that God will arise and give us what we need.

PRAYER

O Lord, may I forgive others that you might forgive me. O Lord, may I give to the needy that you might meet my daily needs. I come today by faith and ask that you fill me with your Holy Spirit as a gift of your grace. Grant unto me the spirit of perseverance that I might prevail in my prayers and requests before you whenever those requests are according to your will. And empower me as well to give unto others the encouragement which you have given to me in Jesus. Amen.

MEDITATION TWENTY-NINE
PRAYER BEFORE THE THRONE OF GRACE

MEDITATION TWENTY-NINE

PRAYER BEFORE

ANOTHER encouragement for a poor, trembling, convicted soul is to consider the place, throne, or seat on which the great God has placed himself to hear the petitions and prayers of poor creatures—and that is the throne of grace or the mercy seat. "Let us then approach the throne of grace with confidence, so that we may receive mercy and find grace to help us in our time of need" (Heb. 4:16).

In these days of the gospel, God has taken up his seat, his abiding-place, in mercy and forgiveness; and from his throne of grace he intends to hear the sinner and to commune with him. Poor souls! They are very apt to entertain strange thoughts of God and his attitude toward them, and suddenly conclude that God will pay no attention to them. Yet he is upon his mercy seat. He has taken up his place on purpose there, to the end that he may hear and regard the prayers of poor creatures. If he had said, "I will commune with you from my throne of judgment," then indeed you might have trembled and fled from the great and glorious majesty. But when he says that he will hear and commune with souls upon the throne of grace, or upon the mercy seat, this should encourage you and cause you to hope. Come boldly to the throne of grace!

As there is a mercy seat from whence God is willing to commune with poor sinners, so there is also by his seat Jesus Christ. Jesus Christ is continually sprinkling the mercy seat with his blood. As Scripture says: "You have come to God, the judge of all men, to the spirits of righteous men made perfect, to Jesus the mediator of a new covenant, and to the sprinkled blood that speaks a better word than the blood of Abel" (Heb. 12:23, 24).

When the Jewish high priest was to go into the Holy of Holies where the mercy seat was, he could not go in without blood (Heb. 9:7). Why so? Because God was on the mercy seat, and he was perfectly just as well as merciful. Now the blood was to stop justice from running out upon the persons concerned in the intercession of the high priest (Lev. 16:13-17). This should signify to you that all your unworthiness should not hinder you from coming to God in Christ for mercy. You cry out that you are sinful, and therefore God will not regard your prayers. It is true, if you delight in your sins and come to God in mere pretense. But if from a sense of your unworthiness you do pour out your heart to God, desiring to be saved from your guilt, and cleansed from all your filth, with all your heart; fear not, for your sinfulness will not cause the Lord to stop his ear from hearing you. The value of the blood of Christ which is sprinkled upon the mercy seat stops the flow of justice, and opens a floodgate for the mercy of the Lord to be extended to you.

Jesus is there before God to sprinkle the mercy seat with his blood. He speaks and his blood speaks. Jesus has an audience, and his blood has an audience; insomuch that God says when he sees the blood, he will pass over you (Exod. 12).

Be sober and humble. Go to the Father in the name of his Son and tell him your case. Go in the assistance of the Spirit and with your understanding also in accordance with the Word of God.

PRAYER

Dear heavenly Father, Father of light and truth, I thank you that during this time when the gospel is being preached around the world that you are seated upon a mercy seat, the throne of grace. I thank you that I can come to you through the shed blood of Jesus Christ, and that I do not have to feel the threat of deserved judgment because of his intercession for me. Help me now to share this precious Good News that many might be saved through faith. Amen.

MEDITATION THIRTY
DO NOT GRIEVE THE HOLY SPIRIT

THERE is and must be a sad reproof for those who never pray at all. "I will pray," said the Apostle, and so should all Christians. You are not a Christian if you are not a praying person. The promise of God is that everyone who is righteous will pray: "Therefore let everyone who is godly pray to you while you may be found; surely when the mighty waters rise, they will not reach him" (Ps. 32:6). You then are a wicked person if you do not pray!

Jacob got the name of Israel by wrestling with God in prayer: "Then the man said, 'Your name will no longer be Jacob, but Israel, because you have struggled with God and with men and have overcome' " (Gen. 32:28). And all of his children have borne that name with him: "Peace and mercy to all who follow this rule, even to the Israel of God" (Gal. 6:16).

But the people who forget prayer, who call not upon the name of the Lord, they have prayers made for them, but they are prayers such as this: "Pour out your wrath on the nations that do not acknowledge you, *on the peoples who do not call on your name*" (Jer. 10:25). Are you like these people who do not call upon the name of the Lord?

136

Do you go to bed like a dog and rise like a hog, or a sot, and forget to call upon God? What will you do when you are damned in hell, because you could not find it in your heart to pray to God and ask for heaven? Who will be there to grieve for your sorrow, because you didn't count the mercy of God worth asking for? You have not the heart to ask for heaven or approach our great God in prayer when he is upon his throne of grace. You must eternally perish in hell if you do not ask God for heaven.

What about you who make it your business to slight, mock at, and undervalue the Spirit and praying by the Holy Spirit? What will you do when God calls you to account for these things? You consider it treason to speak a word against a government official. Indeed, you tremble at the thought of it. Yet in the meantime you blaspheme the Spirit of the Lord. Is God indeed to be trifled with, and will the end be pleasant for you? Did God send the Holy Spirit into the hearts of his people so that they could taunt him, especially when he calls them to prayer? Is this to serve God? Does this demonstrate the reformation of your church? Can you be content to be damned for your sins against the law, and can you add to this your sin against the Holy Spirit?

Must the holy, harmless and undefiled Spirit of grace, the nature of God, the promise of Christ, the Comforter of his children, the one without whom no one can be acceptable to the Father—must this, I say, be the burden of your song, to taunt, deride, and mock at him? If God sent Korah and his company headlong into hell for speaking against Moses and Aaron, do you who mock the Spirit of Christ think you can escape unpunished (see Num. 16 and Heb. 10)? Did you never read what God did to Ananias and Sapphira for telling just one lie to the Holy Spirit (Acts 5)? What about Simon Magus, who undervalued the Spirit and his work (Acts 8)? And will your sin be a virtue, or go unrewarded with vengeance, if you make it your business to rage against and oppose his office, service and help that he gives to the children of God in prayer? It is a fearful thing to oppose and despise the Spirit of grace, for the Spirit would bless your life and your prayers.

As this is the doom of those who do openly blaspheme the Holy Spirit, in a day of disdain and reproach to his office and service, so also it is sad for you who resist the spirit of prayer by relying on rituals and written prayers to bring you close to God. A very juggle of the Devil, that the traditions and rituals of men should be better esteemed than the spirit of heartfelt prayer. Is this any less than the accursed abomination of Jeroboam, who kept many from going to Jerusalem, the place and way of God's appointment to worship? One would think that God's judgments of old upon the hypocrites of that day would make those who have heard of it take heed and fear to do the same. Yet the religious teachers of our day are so far from taking the warning of this punishment of others that they most desperately rush into the same transgression by placing their traditions above the Scriptures and their written prayers above praying in the spirit. They set up institutions of men, neither commanded nor commended by God, and then they say that whosoever will not obey them must be run out of the land or executed. Thus is the spirit of prayer disowned, and the form of the printed prayer *imposed*. The Spirit is debased, and the manmade form of prayer is extolled. Those who pray with the Spirit, though ever so humble and holy, are counted as fanatics. Those who pray with the form of a written prayer only, and without the Spirit, are counted virtuous. And how will those in favor of such a practice answer that Scripture which commands that the church turn away from such people who have a form of godliness and deny the power of it (2 Tim. 3:5)?

God is ever ready to give us the spirit of prayer. His Holy Spirit is always seeking to persuade us to pray for those blessings he wants to give us and others. Let us open our hearts and minds to God and ask him to fill us with his Spirit and a burning desire to pray for showers of blessing.

PRAYER

O Lord, I live in a different time from that of John Bunyan, who was forced by law and by the church's authorities to pray and worship you in a certain manner and formality, and who was imprisoned for his disobedience. And yet I find that the temptation is always before me to honor men and the works of men far more than you. Forgive me for those times when I have rejected the influence of the Holy Spirit, who was calling me from sin and to prayer. Today, I resolve to be sensitive to his leading, so I can pray to you at his bidding. Amen.

MEDITATION THIRTY-ONE
PUT GOD BEFORE MAN

HE who advances the *Book of Common Prayer* or any book of church ritual above the spirit of prayer advances a form of men's prayer above the Holy Spirit's leading and influence. Such people banish, or desire to banish, those who pray with the spirit of prayer, while they embrace and applaud those who pray with the form only, and that because they use the *Book of Common Prayer.* Therefore they love and advance the form of their own or others' inventing before the spirit of prayer, which is God's special and gracious appointment.

Look into the jails of England and into the barrooms and I know that you will find those who plead for the spirit of prayer in the jails, while those who defend books of ritual can be found walking freely in the streets or in the barrooms. It is evident also by the silencing and jailing of God's dear ministers, though ever so powerfully enabled by the spirit of prayer, if they in conscience cannot subscribe to that form of written prayer. This is clearly an exalting of the *Book of Common Prayer* above either praying by the Spirit or preaching the Word. It is not pleasant for me to dwell on this. May the Lord in mercy turn the hearts of the people to seek more after the spirit of prayer and, in the strength of that, to pour out their souls before the Lord. Only let me say it is a sad sign that that which is one of the most eminent parts of the pretended worship of God is anti-Christian when it has nothing but the tradition of men and the strength of persecution to uphold or plead for it.

I shall conclude with a word of advice to all God's people.

1. Believe that as surely as you walk in the ways of God you will meet with temptations.

2. The first day therefore that you enter into Christ's congregation, look for temptations to come.

3. When temptations do come, beg of God to carry you through them.

4. Be jealous of your own heart, and do not let it deceive you in your evidences of heaven or in your walking with God in this world.

5. Take heed of the flatteries of false brethren.

6. Keep in the life and power of the truth.

7. Look most at the things which are not seen.

8. Take heed of little sins.

9. Keep the promise of God warm upon your heart.

10. Renew your acts of faith in the blood of Christ.

11. Consider the work God has for your generation.

12. Resolve to run with the foremost of the godly of your generation.

Grace be with you.

THE SPIRIT OF PRAYER

Wouldst thou have that good, that blessed mind,
That is so much to heavenly things inclin'd
That it aloft will soar, and always be
Contemplating on the blest eternity.
That mind that never thinks itself at rest,

But when it knows it is forever blest;
That mind that can be here no more content,
Than he that in the prison doth lament;
That blessed mind that counts itself then free
When it can at the throne with Jesus be,
There to behold the mansions he prepares
For such as be with him and his co-heirs.
This mind is in the covenant of grace,
*And shall be theirs that truly seek his face.**

PRAYER

O Lord, my God and Savior, may I be strengthened by your Spirit and by all that I have learned from John Bunyan, who suffered intense and lengthy persecution for his faith. May I be strengthened in my mind by the words of teaching and admonition he has proclaimed from the Scriptures, that I might love you with all of my mind. May I be strengthened in soul and spirit by your Spirit of truth working in my life, that I might love you with all my mind and soul and strength. May I be strengthened in my heart whenever I am tempted to place the traditions of men above your Word and Spirit. Strengthen me and fill me with your Spirit so I can better and more courageously witness to others about your redeeming love and the life transforming power of your gospel. For the sake of your kingdom. Amen.

*From "Ebal and Gerizim," a long poem by Bunyan.

JOHN BUNYAN'S
DYING WORDS ON PRAYER

Before you enter into prayer, ask your soul these questions:

1. To what end, O my soul, am I retired into this place? Am I come to discourse with the Lord in prayer? Is he present, will he hear me? Is he merciful, will he help me? Is my business with him unimportant? Is it concerning the welfare of my soul? What words will I use to move him to compassion?

2. To make your preparation complete, consider that you are but dust and ashes, and he is the great God and Father of our Lord Jesus Christ. He clothes himself with light as with a garment, and you are but a sinner. He is a holy God, and you are but a sinful creature. He is the omnipotent Creator.

3. In all your prayers do not forget to thank God for all of his mercies.

4. When you pray, rather let your heart be without words than your words be without heart.

5. Prayer will make a man cease from sin or sin will entice a man to cease from prayer.

6. The spirit of prayer is more precious than treasures of gold and silver.

7. Pray often, for prayer is a shield to the soul, a sacrifice to God, and a scourge to Satan.

THE LORD'S PRAYER IN VERSE

Our Father which in heaven art,
  Thy name be always hallowed;
Thy kingdom come, thy will be done:
  Thy heavenly path be followed
  By us on earth as 'tis with thee,
    We humbly pray;
  And let our bread us given be,
    From day to day.
Forgive our debts as we forgive
  Those that to us indebted are:
Into temptation lead us not,
  But save us from the wicked snare.
The kingdom's thine, the power too.
  We thee adore:
The glory also shall be thine
  For evermore.

By John Bunyan
Date unknown

MANSOUL'S PETITION
TO EMMANUEL

O Lord and Sovereign Prince Emmanuel, the potent, the long-suffering Prince: grace is poured into Thy lips, and to Thee belongs mercy and forgiveness, though we have rebelled against Thee. We who are no more worthy to be called Thy Mansoul, nor yet fit to partake of common benefits, do beseech Thee, and Thy Father by Thee to do away our transgressions. We confess that Thou mightest cast us away for them, but do it not for Thy name's sake; let the Lord rather take an opportunity at our miserable condition, to let out His bowels and compassions to us; we are compassed on every side, Lord, our own backslidings reprove us; our Diabolonians within our town fright us, and the army of the angel of the bottomless pit distresses us. Thy grace can be our salvation, and whither to go but to Thee we know not.

Furthermore, O gracious Prince, we have weakened our captains, and they are discouraged, sick, and of late some of them grievously worsted and beaten out of the field by the power and force of the tyrant. Yea, even those of our captains in whose valour we did formerly use to put most of our confidence, they are as wounded men. Besides

Lord, our enemies are lively, and they are strong, they vaunt and boast themselves, and do threaten to part us among themselves for a booty. They are fallen also upon us, Lord, with many thousand doubters, such as with whom we cannot tell what to do; they are all grim-looked, and unmerciful ones, and they bid defiance to us and Thee.

Our wisdom is gone, our power is gone, because Thou art departed from us, nor have we what we may call ours but sin, shame, and confusion of face for sin. Take pity upon us, O Lord, take pity upon us, Thy miserable town of Mansoul, and save us out of the hands of our enemies. Amen.

From John Bunyan's *The Holy War*
First published in 1682*

*Since this prayer probably represents the way John Bunyan himself prayed, we include it here in the original words.

A NOTE ON THE TEXT

The material on prayer in this book is taken from *The Whole Works of John Bunyan,* edited by George Offor and published in London by Blackie and Sons in 1875. The meditations are taken from the discourse "On Praying in the Spirit." In editing the thirty-one meditations, I have completely modernized the text, shortened sentences, and changed obsolete words, such as the word *vizard.* The meditation titles are my own, as well as the divisions into the thirty-one meditations. In many cases, I have quoted Bunyan's Scripture references entirely where it has proved helpful. I believe the text is true to what Bunyan would want it to be for the twentieth-century reader, and I hope that the devotional format will attract more readers of Bunyan's fine material on prayer than otherwise would have been the case.

SCRIPTURE INDEX